Blade Runner

Scene-by-Scene

Walter Adam
2019

Blade Runner

Scene-by-Scene

John David Ebert

ISBN: 978-0-9971356-0-2

Post Egoism Media | Eugene, Oregon

Acknowledgements

Special thanks go to JD Casten for his outstanding design and layout, as usual. Also Tom Ebert and Lawrence Pearce for his fantastic cover art.

Cover artwork:
"Los Angeles 2019" (2015) by Lawrence Pearce

Contents

Acknowledgements   5

Introduction: On the Late Stage World City   11

(2007 Final Cut: 0:00 – 2:59)
Opening Crawl   19

(2:59 – 4:14)
The Hades Cityscape   23

(4:15 – 7:25)
Holden and Kowalski   27

(7:25 – 11:03)
Deckard's Ascent   33

(11:03 – 15:39)
Bryant   39

(15:39 – 22:39)
Rachael   47

(22:40 – 25:04)
Kowalski's Apartment   55

(25:05 – 30:20)
Chew's Eye Works   59

(30:21 – 36:19)
Rachael and Deckard   65

(36:19 – 41:30)
Pris and J.F. Sebastian   71

(41:30 – 47:38)
Snake Scale   75

(47:38 - 59:26)
Zhora   79

(59:32 – 62:77)
Leon and Deckard   85

(62:77 – 72:42)
Rachael and Deckard (Redux)   89

(72:42 – 79:74)
Pris, Sebastian and Roy   95

(79:74 – 86:55)
Tyrell   101

(86:56 – 93:64)
The "Retirement" of Pris   107

(93:65 – 108:67)
The Battle with Roy   111

(108:67 – 111:83)
Rescuing Rachael   119

Epilogue
Escape to the Countryside   121

End Notes   123

Bibliography   127

Introduction:

On the Late Stage World City

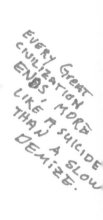

Ridley Scott's vision of Los Angeles in 2019 AD is not a city of the future, but rather a type of city that emerges near the end phase of a civilization when huge urban agglomerations have come in to replace provincial capitals of culture like Athens, Bruges or Florence.[1] Scott's Los Angeles is simply a larger scale version of today's global world cities, but these cities are, on a turn of the historical spiral, retrievals of the ancient type of world city cosmopolis configured by Rome, Byzantium or Alexandria.

Huge and impersonal, such cities are characterized by enormous population swarms, many of which are composed of landless farmers or soldiers who have returned home from wars only to find their lands bought out by the agribusiness corporations known as *latifundia*. These *latifundia* developed after the Punic Wars and began to spring into being around the 2nd century BC in places like Magna Graecia, Spain, Sicily and North Africa, and they depended almost entirely upon slaves for their gigantic output of agricultural exports, such as olive oil, grain or wine. These were the ancient equivalents of today's multi-national corporations, especially such agri-business corporations like Monsanto, for they, too, gobbled up all the nearby private farms and sent their desperate owners migrating to the world cities looking for work, just like the soldiers returning home from the wars, only to find that their lands had been acquired by men of wealth such

Agrigarian Cultures soon evolved into corporate based oligoarchies — Land became a luxury of the rich.

as Crassus. Consequently, these ancient world cities swelled in numbers and became massive, extensive operations often requiring stupendous feats of engineering—such as the construction of huge aqueducts and gladiatorial arenas—to manage them. The populations of these world cities, then, were composed of multi-ethnic swarms who had poured in from all corners of the Empire, robbed of their lands and transformed into nomads migrating to the cities in search of employment.

Such cities can be characterized as rootless, "worldless" in the Heideggerian sense, and entirely artificial. The human swarm, that formless mass of social *dis*-organization, came into being as their side effect, and special tenement buildings known as *insulae* ("island")—multi-story apartment structures—had to be invented to accommodate these population swarms. Such buildings, needless to say, were cheaply built out of mud-brick and timber and often collapsed during earthquakes. They were places of squalor, filth and overcrowding that were owned by men of wealth like Crassus, who made his fortunes off of acquiring such real estate. (Donald Trump comes to mind as his modern equivalent). *BASELESS GREED LEADING TO SOCIETAL COLLAPSE*

The wealthy classes lived in single family residences called *domi*, replete with marble statues, inlaid marble paneling and elaborate frescoes, paintings and fountains. They also had carefully cultivated gardens, indoor courtyards and atriums. Their front entrances, needless to say, were turned *away* from the crowded streets of Rome, for the *domi* were not normally segregated into their own neighborhoods but situated in the midst of the squalid *insulae* housing the poor.

These kinds of world cities, as I have said, are products of the late stages of their respective societies, and their concerns are almost entirely post-metaphysical, for their intellectuals are preoccupied with politics, economics and ethics. Life in such world cities is no longer lived spontaneously and lyrically, but has be-

12

come a problem to be solved. Hence, such birth control methods as infanticide and abortion are routine, despite the overcrowding, for the life instinct no longer expresses itself with confidence and certainty, since existence in such world cities has become overburdened with problems.

These cities, as Oswald Spengler has pointed out, have come to replace the earlier phase cultural capitals like Athens, Florence or Weimar, small, livable places that once gave rise to the arts and where metaphysical concerns had been paramount. By the time of the late phase world city, such small scale towns are thought of as "provincial," and looked down upon by the world weary intellectuals—inevitably atheist, skeptical, irreligious—of the megalopolis.[2] Thus, in the shift from the early provincial culture capital to the late period of the cosmopolis—say, from Munich to Berlin—there occurs a shift in cultural values from metaphysics and religion to atheism, economics and money.

There is, therefore, little that is new in Ridley Scott's vision of an overcrowded, multi-ethnic Los Angeles of 2019, save for the scale of it: 20 million people are said to dwell there, and the city is a labyrinth from which there is no apparent escape, for it has become a world island unto itself. Also novel is that it has become lit from within like a Christmas tree, plugged in and turned on, with electric current racing through it and powering its various neon signs, billboards and advertisements.

The city in *Blade Runner*, furthermore, is composed of de-worlded signifiers that have been cut loose from all local contexts and set into circulation through the global metabolism. Hence, the Japanese Noodle Bar; the bicycle-riding Chinamen; the German-speaking street gangs; the Indian Hare Krishnas; the Cambodian street vendor; the Arabic snake merchant: all have been cut free from the contexts of their originating world horizons and let loose into the global metabolism. They are signs allowed to circulate and proliferate inside Scott's cosmopolitan

Los Angeles, where they float, drift, crash and collide into one another without aim or purpose.[3] As a result, nihilism prevails and metaphysics is non-existent.[4]

The absence of a structuring metaphysic to function as an apparatus of capture with which to nail the signs in place allows for the disintegration of all ethical values that would put a stop to, or restrain, the genetic engineering of artificial humans. Science and technology reign here; art and metaphysics are relics from a bygone past of local horizons and places where, as Heidegger put it, things *thing* and worlds *world*.[5] The Los Angeles of 2019 is a worldless city where the transnational corporation holds sway and a weakened state can do nothing to stop its "advances," but can barely keep up with its technological innovations, such as the Nexus 6 generation of Replicant designed to outsmart the Voigt-Kampff test created by the police to probe Replicants for the absence of emotional affect. Replicants with emotions are a novelty that renders such a test obsolete. *That* is the crisis of the film: technology cannot be stopped, slowed down or reversed, for it is liquefying all cultural values with each new advance that renders them antiquated and so allows nihilism to prevail.

The difference engine that drives the narrative of *Blade Runner* is composed of the binarity—and there are many of them, as the following analysis will reveal—of the Tyrell Corporation headquarters and the crumbling apartment building inhabited by J.F. Sebastian. For whereas the Tyrell Corporation manufactures slave labor for its modern day Off-world *latifundia*, Sebastian's tenement is a post-historic equivalent of an ancient Roman *insula*: a place of squalor, darkness and maximal entropy. Everything that finds its way to his derelict building, goes there *to die*.

Origin, Eros, Evolution, then: these are the ideas associated with Tyrell and his bioengineered humans. Entropy, decay, obsolescence: these, in turn, characterize Sebastian's residence.

SLAVES

[handwritten margin note: while maintaining a desire to find humanity and to LIVE]

14

Tyrell's headquarters are of course a modern *domus*, and he himself is an equivalent of the ancient Roman men of wealth, while his chess game opponent, J.F. Sebastian—who does some genetic design work for him—inhabits his modern day *insula* as its sole occupant. The Tyrell Corporation, however, is a contemporary equivalent of the massive *latifundia* which bought out private farms and divested people of their ties to the soil, uprooting them and sending them to the giant mega-machine cities looking for work. Tyrell himself owns a monopoly, not on land, but on the rights to bioengineer slave labor to work the exoplanetary colonies.

The rebellion of the Nexus 6 Replicants, then, is equivalent to a kind of miniature Spartacus slave revolt, for the Replicants, like the ancient slaves, constitute an internal proletariat that is *in* the society though not *of* it, since they have no rights and are illegal on earth. Which is to say that they are "unhomed" ontologically speaking, for they can claim no metaphysical world island to shelter them. They are unprotected by any macrosphere—only Tyrell's headquarters, where they are manufactured, can afford them any safe zone of habitation, however momentary—and exist on the ontological level of Giorgio Agamben's *zoe*, or "bare naked life," for they, too, like concentration camp refugees such as Bosnian Muslims, Palestinians or Darfurians, can be killed with impunity.[6]

Caught in between this difference engine of the Tyrell Corporation and J.F. Sebastian's crumbling *insula* is the Blade Runner named Rick Deckard, whose job is to *unmake* the artificial humans which Tyrell generates from out of the metaphysical vulva that he has appropriated from the Great Mother. Deckard, in fact, will find himself caught in between a whole series of metaphysical dichotomies—authentic human vs. Replicant, to name one—which the narrative will gradually deconstruct. Deckard, as my analysis will show, will slowly find these binarities collapsing into each other—like one of Derrida's deconstructions in *Of Grammatology*—to the point where his once metaphysically structured universe of pure bivalencies will decay into so many "undecidables" that existence within the world city of Los Angeles will become impossible for him any longer. Escape from the world island of 2019 Los Angeles—together with his modern Eurydice, the Nexus 6 Replicant known as Rachael—will eventually become his main goal. Even the binarity of Tyrell's headquarters vs. Sebastian's *insula* will collapse when Roy Batty reterritorializes Sebastian's tenement into a gladiatorial arena during the film's last half hour.

The collapse and decay of all metaphysical structures into post-metaphysical undecidables is what *Blade Runner* is all about.

See for yourself.

A Note on the Various Film Versions

As is well known, there are many different versions of Blade Runner—almost too many to count—from the original Workprint to the 2007 Final Cut. Though I refer to these other versions when and where they are necessary to shed light on certain meaning structures in the narrative, I have used the 2007 Final Cut—despite its flaws—as my primary text for analysis, simply because it is the most recent and "final" version. So all the time stamps refer to that version of the film, but I have found the Workprint version that surfaced in 1990 at the Fairfax Film Festival to be especially useful for some of the deeper elucidations. That version is difficult to find, but it is the most dramatically "different" version from the original Theatrical Release and is worth the effort to track down simply in order to perform an "archaeology" on the film's thematic and narrative evolution.

Besides, nowadays we've got the Internet. What more do we need?

Opening Crawl

As the title credits file past to the first synthesizer tones of Vangelis's score, at about 2:05, a vertical crawl begins to slide up the screen from bottom to top, a crawl which informs the film's audience that the Tyrell Corporation has advanced robotic evolution into a Nexus 6 phase. These "robots," however, are not quite exactly robots, since they are genetically engineered and therefore made out of biological material—i.e. cells, genes, bones—by the Tyrell Corporation. They are thus technically termed "Replicants," as the crawl informs us.

Replicants are illegal on earth, especially after a violent mutiny occurred in an Off-world colony, and their presence on the planet is an immediate death sentence. Blade Runner units are special police forces designed to shoot to kill, upon detection, any Replicant that is found on earth, although, as the crawl informs us, this was not called "execution" but rather "retirement."

A Blade Runner retires, but does not "kill" a Replicant, since a Replicant is not to be regarded as a "real" human being, but a convincing "replica" of a human being. Viruses replicate; bacteria replicate; cells replicate; but humans "reproduce." In other words, humans are not simply clones of one another, but biological singularities that constitute "difference" rather than "repetition." A "Replicant," on the other hand, is a repetition, or merely a "repeat" of a human being, but not the real thing. (Coca-cola, however, insists—as it always has—that *it* is "the real thing," or in other words the authentic capitalist consumer product that

19

is capable of mass reproduction and global dissemination. It is however, *not* a real [i.e. "natural"] thing at all, but a chemically produced soft drink that was dreamed up by a pharmacist in his Atlanta basement.)

It is significant, then, that the Tyrell Corporation—this monolithic transnational entity that appears to have a monopoly on synthetic humans—is located in Los Angeles, of all places, the capital of hyperreality where phantasmatic humans are produced every day. A celebrity, for instance, is not "the real thing," either, but a replicated human which depends upon a mediatic substrate, what theoretician Boris Groys calls a "sign carrier" across which media signifiers may be displayed and which they presuppose in order to exist.[7] A celebrity is a replicated human being who cannot exist without some kind of "medial sign carrier" such as film, radio, television or nowadays, of course, the Internet. (The "sign-carrier," or mediatic substrate, which the existence of a Replicant presupposes is, on the *narrative* level, biological matter [cells, genes, DNA] but on the mediatic level it is celluloid and in Dick's novel, the printed book).

Silicon Valley—and here, we should note that the novel was originally located in San Francisco, but moved to Los Angeles by director Ridley Scott due to logistical reasons—has also now made it possible to democratize the cult and culture of celebrity by making available to all and sundry the possibility of creating electronic duplicates of ourselves using such technologies as Internet web sites, smart phones and iPads.[8]

So, though on one level, the film will treat the surface theme of genetic engineering and its tragic consequences (such as genetic pollution), the deeper levels of Scott's narrative involve an exploration of the Californian replication and replacement of reality by the fake, the clone, the avatar. If one then extends this *Kulturkreiss*—or zone of distribution of a cultural signifier—to Tokyo, with all its Idorus, Anime figures and Manga, then it be-

20

comes clear that Scott's film is also, in the wider sense, an exploration of the significance of Pacific Rim-based electronic hyperreality.[9] (Whereas one would expect the center of genetic engineering corporations to be located on the North American East Coast, where, amongst the decaying ruins of the Industrial Rust Belt such research is mostly conducted nowadays. So it can be said that the American East Coast is the center for the manipulation of *physical* matter—whether genes or machines—just as the West Coast is the center for the manipulation of technologies of light and illusion, or *subtle* matter).

A further point regarding the opening crawl: whereas the Tyrell Corporation manufactures its Replicants for Off-world usage as slave labor, it must make them *on earth*, in Los Angeles— in Dick's novel, the Tyrell Corporation, there called the Rosen Association, is located in Seattle—from whence it exports them to the *Transcendenz* of the Off-world colonies where they are legal. (They are illegal on earth because they lack the capacity for empathy, and are therefore dangerous, since they regard human beings the same way human beings regard insects: as nuisances to be squashed at will). They are "inauthentic" humans because they have not only been (presumably) grown in labs at the Tyrell Corporation, but they have only four year life spans. They also possess extreme, superhero-like abilities of strength and agility that make them especially dangerous to humans on earth, but useful in the hazardous undertaking of colonizing other planets.

The Tyrell Corporation, then, creates its Replicants on earth, and exports them off the planet to other worlds. They are therefore, strictly speaking—and as Dick's novel points out—only legal on the premises of the Tyrell Corporation. If they are caught outside the Tyrell Corporation—which thus functions for them as a Zone of Habitability—they are to be terminated by Blade Runner police.

But Advertised as "More Human Than Human."

So, in other words, a Blade Runner functions like a white blood cell: his job is to identify the infected area and fight the infection by any means at his disposal. Replicants are, indeed, then, viral. Their presence on earth—or at least within the cosmopolis of Los Angeles—is tantamount to an infection and a Blade Runner is therefore sent to wipe out the infection by terminating the Replicant, this synthetic human that is not allowed within the city precincts of Los Angeles, even though it has been permitted to be manufactured there.

Blade Runners—in Dick's novel they are merely "bounty hunters" who collect large sums of money for killing "androids"—are thus the white blood cells of the city of Los Angeles. But they are only tasked with keeping fake *humans* out; fake *animals* are allowed. In Dick's novel—and by implication in Scott's film—almost all animals on earth have been wiped out by a nuclear war, for there exists a permanent gray haze surrounding the planet which blocks out the sunlight. Only the city functions as a kind of macrosphere inside which the human survives like an exotic pet in a terrarium lit with a grimy fluorescent tube. (In Scott's film, there is no indication of a nuclear war, but rather some sort of ecocide in which human industrial engineering has covered the planet with a gigantic city that has replaced all things natural with pure artifice. Living animals have, therefore, become a thing of the past, and their simulacra are most welcome as nostalgic reminiscences. Indeed, in the novel, Rick Deckard's motivation for tracking down the escaped Nexus 6 "androids" is to save up enough money to buy a real live animal [a horse] to replace the robotic sheep which he keeps on his rooftop).

THE OPPOSITE OF A HUNTER KILLING A LIVE DEER TO GET A TROPHY

22

(2:59 – 4:14)
The Hades Cityscape

A title card now appears onscreen, informing the audience that the story is set in Los Angeles in the year 2019. A vast, industrial cityscape then emerges into view, a cityscape that extends with spires and towers to a distant vanishing point on the pink horizon beneath which the sun has just set. As the camera drifts across this cityscape—called by the film's production designers, "Hades"[10]—huge blooms of fire erupt from the industrial smokestacks of factories, while hovercars come roaring past the viewer, and toward two distant skyscrapers. As the camera floats across this sea of buildings—to the dreamlike synth score of Vangelis's music—it becomes more and more clear that they are headed for the two buildings which are shaped like Mesopotamian ziggurats. These buildings, which tower over every other structure, happen to be the headquarters of the Tyrell Corporation (indeed, they invite a certain comparison with the twin temples of the Templo Mayor pyramids of Aztec Tenochtitlan), where a Blade Runner named Dave Holden has just been sent to perform the so-called Voigt-Kampff empathy test upon some of its recent employees, in an attempt to uncover any of the escaped Nexus 6 Replicants.

Note that the cityscape is composed of signifiers that *fold in*—in the Derridean sense in which one text can be folded into another—three different epochs of technological development: the spires belching flame in the foreground signify the Industrial Revolution, whereas the glittering sea of lights indicates the Electric—and also electronic—Revolution at the end of the nineteenth century in which all our cities were plugged in and turned on for the first time. The Tyrell buildings, then, are metonyms for the biotechnological revolution which is currently in its early, and still formative, phases. All three phases (industrial, electric, biotechnological)—historically unfolding in diachronic sequence—are in the film's opening image, thus folded—like a macroscale piece of one of Gaff's origami—into a space of simultaneity, one inside the other, where they compose the very fabric of the Hadean cityscape.

It is appropriate that the production design team nicknamed the city "Hades," after the Greek underworld, for the city in *Blade Runner* is a vast apparatus of capture from whence—just like the Greek underworld—*no* signifiers are allowed to escape. It is an Anti-Sphere, to use Peter Sloterdijk's term,[11] one that has overcoded and effaced all signs of earthly vegetation and animal life. Indeed, it is a vast horizontal cathedral with industrial spires and electronic stained glass that has captured *all* human beings; human beings whose only chance of escape from the labyrinth is exclusively *vertical*, that is, for one to qualify for relocation to an Off-world colony.

It is also significant that the film opens just after the sun has set, for almost the entire story, which unfolds over the course of a number of days, takes place at night. Dick's novel, on the other hand, transpires over the course of twenty-four hours and begins with Rick Deckard and his wife Iran waking up in the morning and ends with them going to bed the following morning after Deckard has spent the entire night chasing down and terminating the escaped Nexus 6 androids. The story is, therefore—in the now archaic jargon of comparative mythology—a "night sea journey" through the Underworld of a cosmopolitan monster city, and so it is extremely important to its semiotic, for precisely this reason, that the penultimate scene of Roy Batty's dove escaping into the blue sky be retained (in the 2007 Final Cut, the blue sky

24

of dawn is [unfortunately] digitally revised to a *night* sky, while the daylight ending of the original 1982 Theatrical Release of Deckard and Rachael driving off into the green, sun-soaked hills has been cut). But, as we will see, the filmmakers, I believe, had it right the first time: for the whole point of the film is that *this* Orpheus will successfully escape from the city-as-underworld with his Eurydice, thereby transforming the Greek myth of the underworld as enclosure into the contemporary post-historic cosmology of the Open Universe, in which there *are* no enclosures, for the planet is now open and ontologically unprotected by any immunizing macrospheres whatsoever. As Peter Sloterdijk once put it: being-in-the-world now means being *thrown* into it, in which a real Outside appears for the first time in cosmological history.[12]

There also occurs, in this sequence, a close-up shot of a huge human eye in which the towers of flame are reflected. The eye is framed in a gigantic close-up that has the effect of severing it from the rest of its human anatomy so that it becomes a signifying partial object unto itself, inviting a certain comparison to the ancient Eye of Horus, an eye which Horus lost in a battle with his uncle Set and which grew wings to become the disk of the sun. When the eye was retrieved by the god Thoth and returned to Horus, he took it to his dead father's body—that of Osiris—and shone it upon him like a ray of the sun, whereupon it resurrected him. The eye, therefore, in this opening montage—though according to Ridley Scott it was meant to have an Orwellian semiotic—suggests one of the film's primary thematic concerns: that, namely, of the quest for immortality. The dead Osiris, lest we forget, *is given more life* by the Eye of Horus, and that is precisely what the Nexus 6 Replicants, who have returned to earth, are seeking.

That the Tyrell skyscrapers are not at all shaped like traditional skyscrapers but suggest rather the triangular shape of an ancient Mesopotamian ziggurat is not an accident either, for the ziggurat was the meeting place of Heaven and Earth: humans ascended their steep staircases in order to commune with the gods in a temple located at the top, down to which the gods would descend from the stars in order to meet them.

Notice, however, that in *Blade Runner*, the semiotics are reversed: whereas the ancient Immortals of Mesopotamian theology—the creators of human beings—came down to the earth from the heavens to meet their mortal human beings which they initially created to be slaves for them in order to do all their work—ploughing fields, digging canals, etc.—in Ridley Scott's film the Maker is located at the top of his corporation-as-ziggurat on the earth, while the mortal creatures that he has made utilizing the science of genetic engineering come *down* from the heavens to meet with him in order to request *more life*.

In other words, in post-historic society, once the earth has been orbited by human beings, up has become the new down. To an astronaut in outer space, there *are* no directions: up, down and sideways are useless vectors. To post-historic humanity, in which life is lived at the speed of light, perspectival space has been dismantled, and there is only instantaneity: the real time provided by our globalizing communications technologies and the ubiquity of making the near far and the far near, as Heidegger dismissively referred to such technologies.[13]

One must now travel *downward* to the earth—rather than ascend upward to the heavens—to meet one's Maker, for science has appropriated all the ancient myths and transformed them into physical reality. The gods are now actualized down here, on the physical plane of the earth itself: the Eye of Horus as roving satellites; the creation of life as genetically engineered beings; the Great Father of the metaphysical age now as the God of Biomechanics.

(4:15 – 7:25)
Holden and Kowalski

The next scene takes place inside one of the offices on the upper floors of the Tyrell Corporation building, where the camera shows us Blade Runner Dave Holden standing looking out the window in a haze of blue-lit cigarette smoke. He has been sent to the Tyrell headquarters in order to interview a number of its employees to try and determine whether any of them might be one or another of the four remaining escaped Nexus 6 Replicants (originally there were 6). As a man wearing a short-sleeved T-shirt approaches the row of cubicles, a female voice comes over the intercom announcing that Holden's next subject is one Leon Kowalski, who has been working for a few days in the sanitation department of the Tyrell building.

Leon knocks and Holden motions for him to sit down across the table from him, while he seats himself. Holden's sinister-looking Voigt-Kampff machine then extends its mechanical arm with a red electronic eye at the tip that slides into place, pinpointing one of Leon's eyes on its video monitor in close-up, while the machine appears to breathe using a bellows-like pump.[14]

Leon nervously informs Holden that he has already had an IQ test this year but has not yet had a Voigt-Kampff test, whereupon Holden impatiently cuts him off and tells him that reaction time is a factor in the test and that Kowalski must therefore pay careful attention to the questions.

A video monitor with lines of green data scrawling across its black surface rests on the table between them, and as Holden con-

27

firms Kowalski's address, his Voigt-Kampff machine chirps and squeaks busily as it adjusts itself to Leon's physiognomy. Leon asks him if that question is part of the test, but Holden assures him that it is not and that he is merely warming him up.

Holden then proceeds to ask the first question, in which he tells Leon that he is to imagine himself in a desert, but Leon, still nervous, interrupts him and asks whether this is now the test. Holden, irritated, tells him that it is and then goes on to say that Leon now finds himself in a desert alone, when Leon again cuts him off to specify which desert he is supposed to be in. Holden tells him that it doesn't matter what desert he's in, but Leon wants to know what he's doing there, and so Holden explains that perhaps he is just fed up or maybe wants to be by himself, who knows? He then proceeds with the question: Leon is walking in this hypothetical desert when he finds a tortoise, but Leon again interrupts to ask Holden the definition of a tortoise. Holden asks him if he knows what a turtle is, and Leon tells him that he does, so Holden says that it is the same thing. When Leon says that he has never seen a turtle, Holden looks up at him with impatience and Leon hastens to reassure him that he understands what Holden means.

Holden then tells Leon that he now reaches down to flip the tortoise over on its back, while Leon attempts to interrupt him yet again by asking Holden whether he makes up these questions himself. Holden ignores him and then goes on to say that the turtle is lying on its back in the hot sun, its belly baking, and it cannot right itself without Leon's aid. But Leon is not helping the tortoise and Holden wants to know why. Kowalski, growing angry now, wants to know what Holden means by insinuating that he's not helping the tortoise, and Holden says simply that Leon is just not helping the tortoise to right itself. Then he asks, "Why is that, Leon?"

Leon looks puzzled for a moment, but then Holden leans back, dragging on his cigarette, and tells Leon that in answer to his query, the questions have already been written down for Holden by someone else. Holden then clarifies that the test is composed of questions that are designed to provoke an emotional response.

Holden then moves on to the next question and asks Leon to tell him only the good things that come into his mind when he thinks about his mother. But Leon, leaning forward with his hands beneath the table, calmly informs Holden that he will now proceed to tell him about his mother and shoots him through the table with a gun that he has been hiding beneath it the whole time. The blast rips through Holden's coffee mug and is so powerful that it spins him around in his chair. Leon then stands up and fires again, and the second blast sends Holden, still in his chair, through the wall of the adjacent cubicle, where he smashes into another desk. (The question regarding Leon's mother has particularly irked him since he *has* no mother, only a father, the Great Father, God of Biomechanics, who has appropriated the mother's biogenetic capabilities).

Now, the point of the Voigt-Kampff test—which was invented by Dick and retained from the novel—is that it is designed to "sound out" the human interior with emotionally-toned questions that function as depth probes to determine how empathic the test subject might be. Replicants are incapable of empathy—for either humans or any other living creatures—and so a Replicant's response to such questions will involve things like taking too long for the pupil of the eye to dilate, or a lag in empathic response time (since they can certainly fake empathy, although the reaction time, as in the Jungian word association test, will take longer). The Voigt-Kampff test therefore works by testing for *autonomic* responses, such as the blush response or capillary dilation or chemical pheromones released by the subject from sweating, etc., responses which, in ordinary humans are automatic, but which for Replicants must be faked.

The Voigt-Kampff device is thus a means for testing whether a subject is "hollow" on the inside; that is to say, whether he or she is a true Subject in the Western metaphysical sense. Reiner Schurmann, in his book *Broken Hegemonies*, insisted that "consciousness," or human interiority, has been the primary "hegemonic fantasm" or ruling *arche* of the West since Descartes,[15] and the Voigt-Kampff machine is an ingenious method of testing for the presence of such an interior subjectivity. If the responses are faked or too slow, then one is dealing with one of T.S. Eliot's "Hollow Men," and the test subject must therefore be a Replicant (and accordingly, "retired" immediately).

The thing about Replicants, as the Russian theoretician Boris Groys has pointed out in one of his essays,[16] is that they are the human equivalent of the various ready-mades of contemporary art, in that both Replicants and ready-mades are indistinguishable as art objects from their real world analogues *to the human eye*. A Warhol Brillo Box looks exactly the same as a Brillo Box found on the shelf of a grocery store. The only means of detecting the difference is that Warhol's Brillo Box is put into an entirely different context, that of a museum, and given what Groys terms "art documentation" which *tells* us that it is to be regarded as an art object. Replicants, likewise, cannot be told from actual human beings merely by the eye alone and so they must be given documentation, such as photographs, fake memories, etc. But such documentation is not absolutely necessary, since the Voigt-Kampff test—ironically focusing precisely upon the test subject's eye—can determine the difference by such non-visual cues as inferences to be made about the subject's emotions (or lack thereof). If one wants to determine whether a wall is hollow or solid, one cannot do so using one's eye alone: one must use one's hand to bang on it in order to determine the nature of its

[handwritten marginalia:] CAN A REPLICANT SEE ANOTHER REPLICANT AS A REPLICANT. IE. SEE A LACK OF EMPATHY.

30

interiority. One, in other words, *sounds out* the wall by using non-visual means. (A well-constructed Hollywood movie set is also something that cannot be discerned from its real world analogue by the eye alone, and so the comparison with such a set and a Replicant provides us with a subtle clue to the film's fathoming of the Los Angeles Culture Industry and its generation of hyperreal human clones and avatars).

The contemporary artist Paul Thek—who exhibited along with the Pop Artists of New York in the 1960s—critiqued Pop Art for its shallowness with his various anti-objects and installations; one of his most famous works is called *Meat Piece with Warhol Brillo Box* of 1965. For Thek, Warhol's Brillo Box was too hollow; it lacked an interior, and so he simply took another Brillo Box, turned it over on its side and put a fake resin slab of indeterminate "meat" on the inside of it in order to give it the interiority which he felt it lacked. That was his response to what he felt was the "inauthenticity" and hollowness of Pop Art.

Indeed, the hollowness / interiority dichotomy is one of the main structural polarities of *Blade Runner*, and it is first announced in this opening scene with Holden testing Kowalski for the presence of anything like a human interior world of depths and emotions. Indeed, the toymaker with accelerated decrepitude who appears later on in the film, named J.F. Sebastian, lives inside of a *hollow* building, a darkened, crumbling, lightless skyscraper that is void of all occupants save himself and which, moreover, is located in a part of the city that is full of such vacant buildings.

But the vast majority of the buildings and skyscrapers of *Blade Runner*'s 2019 Los Angeles are not hollow at all, but rather completely illuminated from within. They are explosions of electronic light and self-luminosity (indeed, this whole concept of the city as a self-luminous organism—as bioluminescent as one of those jelly fish from the sea's deepest darknesses—was the contribution of production designer and artist Syd Mead; whereas the overcrowded stacking of modular units that look like they are about to fall over is a vision that comes from French comic book artist Moebius, and especially from his comic strip, serialized in *Heavy Metal* magazine, entitled *The Long Tomorrow*).[17]

Blade Runner's "bioluminescent-city-as-living-organism"— later borrowed by James Cameron for his film *The Abyss*, and also George Lucas for *The Phantom Menace*—should be contrasted with the city in John Carpenter's 1981 film *Escape from New York*, a city which is *not* self-luminous at all, but rather a vision of the world city cosmopolis as a pure empty shell, an excreted exoskeleton that has been left behind by its former occupants and which corresponds to J.F. Sebastian's empty skeleton of an apartment building. (Note that all lights in Sebastian's building come from *outside* of it in the form of searchlights shining *into* it.)

The dichotomies thus far, then: self-luminous skyscrapers / empty buildings; hollow humans / people with interior subjectivities whose consciousness shines *out* through their eyes (it is therefore ironic that Replicants, who are supposed to be hollow on the inside, are given luminous cat's eyes by the director). *These* are the themes already announced in this opening scene of *Blade Runner*, themes which will gradually unfold all their implications and ramifications as the narrative proceeds.

[handwritten: windows]

[handwritten: THE EYE IS THE WINDOW TO THE SOUL.]

Deckard's Ascent

There is also a "peaks and vales" dichotomy running throughout the narrative since, with the previous scene, we had been concerned with Dave Holden interviewing Tyrell employees high up
inside the Tyrell skyscraper, whereas, with the introduction of
Rick Deckard, the perspective now shifts down into the canyons
of the buildings below, where we find Deckard at street level and
out of a job. As the camera descends from a shot of skyscrapers
clustered together as a police "spinner" car zips past, to a ground
view looking up at the "Off-world" colonies blimp—which also
has a blinking red Coca-Cola sign on it—it finally settles near
a blue neon sign of a dragon with a blinking red tongue at the
corner of a Noodle Bar across from which Rick Deckard sits on
the ledge of a window in front of an electronics store reading a
newspaper. Crowds of people—Asian, Hispanic, white, etc.—
carrying umbrellas with luminous white handles file past him as
he reads, while an array of television sets blink to the same grainy,
low-rez image in the window behind him. In that window, a large
round neon disc with the word "Origin" written in Kanji script
on it glows in red against a series of horizontal blue neon tubes.

The neon Kanji disc was created by production designer
Tom Southwell, and it is appropriate that it spells out the word
"Origin," since this concept functions as the film's primary thematic concern. Not only have the Nexus 6 Replicants returned
to earth in quest of their "origins" in the form of Eldon Tyrell,
their Maker, but there will also loom the more subtle question

33

of Deckard's origins himself, especially concerning the possibility of whether he might, or might not be, a Replicant. The film's telos is thus present, as it is with organic life—since the "cause" of the acorn is the tree that pulls on its development from the future as its end goal—at its very beginning as an apparently innocuous signifier.

The voiceover narrative that was elided from the film's Final Cut tells us that Deckard is not just casually reading a newspaper but is actually looking for a job since, as the voiceover points out, "they don't advertise for killers in a newspaper." He has recently quit his job as a Blade Runner and so has cut himself free from the police apparatus and is now detached, a floating signifier drifting across the city's urban technoscape.

Deckard glances up for a moment at the "Off-world colonies" blimp that floats ponderously overhead, its spotlight beams stabbing randomly into the night sky around it as a voice recording announces from it the possibility of attaining the artificial *Transcendenz* of a vertical escape from the city by means of an ascent to the heavens. (In a previous draft of the film known as the Workprint, Deckard's voiceover had explained to the viewer that his wife Iran—whose name is retained from the book—had recently divorced him and run off to the colonies with an Off-worlder; hence his askew glance at the blimp).

The Japanese man at the Noodle Bar then waves Deckard across the sidewalk, which is polished with glossy black sheets of neon-mirroring rain, just as a seat at the bar has vacated for him. Deckard sits down at the crowded, smoky counter and insists that he would like four pieces of sushi (with noodles), but the proprietor, for some reason, insists upon only two. Deckard accedes and waits for his meal.

When it is served to him, he is just about to eat when a policeman taps him on the right shoulder, while another man (named Gaff), talks to him in a street *patois* known as "Cityspeak" from his left. Deckard pretends not to understand what he is saying and motions for the proprietor to interpret, who leans forward and tells him that Gaff is informing him that he is under arrest. Deckard, mouth full of noodles, tells Gaff that he's definitely got the wrong guy, but the proprietor says that Gaff is insisting Deckard is a Blade Runner. Deckard says to "tell him I'm eating," but when he hears Gaff mention the name of his former superintendent, Captain Bryant, he knows that he has no choice but to go along with Gaff.

The two then make their way across the crowded, rain-soaked street and into a glossy police spinner, whereupon Gaff, headset on, proceeds to hit the controls that lift the spinner from the ground. The craft is then shown ascending up into the bulky and luminous realm of the skyscrapers while Vangelis's morphine-like score kicks in and puts the viewer into a hypnotic trance.

Deckard, still eating his noodles, looks out the window, across which tiny miniature rivers of rain squirm, as the spinner floats past huge electronic billboards—one with the face of a Japanese woman taking a birth control pill—and with glowing consumer icons and advertisements visible only from the air. Other police spinners roar past below them, their lights encased in red and blue haloes, as Gaff pilots his spinner down to the circular spire of the police precinct below them. The black disk of the precinct, its surface coated with dots of landing lights like flies, surfaces into view as Gaff expertly sets the spinner down into its landing bay on the gleaming, rain-polished rooftop.

In this sequence, Deckard has been lifted bodily from the city's canyons and carried up through its sheets of rain to the top of a circular structure—which should be contrasted with the triangular shape of the Tyrell building from the previous sequence—where he will receive a mission from his former police chief that will set him upon a path that will ultimately end with his self-imposed exile from the city. The scene is, of course, a technological appropriation of the ancient ascent of the soul to the realm of spirit beings, only in this case, Deckard ascends into the realm of corporate capitalist icons and logos that have replaced the ancient saints and angels with an iconology of mass consumerism all their own. This is the world within which Deckard is presently trapped, and from which he will soon be desperate to find a way out.

The soul, Plato said, is in the form of a circle, and so the circular shape of the police precinct, from which Deckard receives a mission designed to align him with his future destiny—that is, exile from the city, and a change in his either / or attitude regarding the status of Replicants—should alert us to the fact that this particular mission comes from deeper zones within him. Deckard's entire view of his world is about to shift off its axis, for he currently regards Replicants and humans as a simple binary opposition of fake / real. Replicants do not have emotions, whereas people do. Replicants are "hollow," people are subjects.

But by the end of the film, this opposition will begin to deconstruct itself, as Deckard discovers that some Replicants—such as Rachael or Roy Batty—*are* capable of emotional depths and even empathy for others. This will then shift them into the ontological status of Derridean "undecidables," including Deckard himself, as Ridley Scott raises the possibility that, even with all his interior subjective consciousness—with its memories, thoughts and feelings—Deckard might just turn out to be a Replicant, too.

The film thus begins with a series of metaphysically certain binary oppositions—hollow / not-hollow; fake / authentic; Replicant / human—that it ends by deconstructing to the status of "undecidables." By the narrative's conclusion, the viewer will be left with a series of broken bi-valencies, shattered into pieces all around him, and with nothing ontologically certain to cling to. This is one reason, perhaps, for why the film was initially so

36

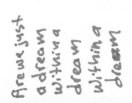

Are we just a dream within a dream within a dream

What is Reality?

unpopular with mass audiences, who do not tend to like ambiguities and prefer their truths to be given to them as metaphysical certainties.

Deckard himself, as well as Rachael, will end as entities with ontologically uncertain categories which the viewer can only tentatively assign to them and which will raise more questions than answers.

Bryant

The next scene, continuing the downward vector of the police spinner's landing, begins with a falling tracking shot—as though the camera has dropped through the roof—that shows the (mostly) vacant and disheveled interior of the vast police station, and then keeps falling until it lands inside Captain Bryant's tiny office, cluttered with fans, dead television sets, and a desk full of inert microphones where the captain is reviewing a report. Deckard comes slamming into the office, and Bryant greets him upon entry, telling him that he knew very well Deckard would not have showed up if Bryant had just asked him to. Deckard hovers in the doorway, however, hesitating a moment before Bryant tells him not to be an asshole and that he's got four "skin-jobs" walking the streets.

Deckard, with Gaff behind him, seats himself in front of Bryant's desk, while the captain pours a couple of shots of liquor (both for Deckard, as Bryant's stomach is shot) as he explains to Deckard that the four skin-jobs jumped an Off-world shuttle and killed all its passengers and crew. The shuttle, he further explains, was found drifting in space, indicating that the Replicants must be on earth somewhere. Deckard, reaching for one of his drinks, simply comments that the episode is an embarrassment, but Bryant corrects him by saying that it's *not* an embarrassment, since Deckard will be assigned to find the four Replicants and kill them before anyone discovers what has happened. Deckard, finishing only one of the drinks and replacing the empty cup on Bryant's desk beside the other (full) one, says that he doesn't work for Bryant anymore and tells him to give the mission to Holden, who is also very good.

But Bryant says that he has already tried that and Holden can still breathe all right only so long as no one unplugs him. He insists that he needs Deckard's expertise on this one, but Deckard still defers, rising to his feet as he says that he was quick when he worked for Bryant and that he's twice as quick now. But Bryant tells him to stop right where he is and explains to him that he is not "cop" but rather "little people."

Gaff, meanwhile, seated in an armchair beside a musty filing cabinet, has spent the scene making a tiny origami chicken out of a piece of discarded cigarette rolling paper, which he now places delicately beside the ashtray as an interesting image of entropy reversal. Indeed, Gaff spends the entire film making his own Replicants out of tiny pieces of discarded waste, as a miniaturization of the film's larger narrative theme of the replacement of the Real with the simulacrum. Gaff's tiny animals are nostalgic signifiers that attempt to fill the gap in the story's symbolic universe once occupied by living animals with his own artificial reminiscences of their presence.

Deckard, having hesitated at the doorway, then walks back to Bryant's desk, realizing that he has no choice (Bryant's ambiguous statement, the viewer surmises—and which is confirmed by Deckard's voiceover in the Workprint scene in which Gaff is flying him to Tyrell's office—was a veiled threat on Deckard's life).

In the next scene, Bryant and Deckard are seated in chairs in an anteroom, this one soaked in smoky blue Venetian lattice light that floods in through the window behind them. They are watching a video of Holden's interview with Leon Kowalski and Kowalski's subsequent attempt at murdering him. The grainy monitor that features Kowalski's dialogue is embedded in a larger electronic console that frames it between a pair of azure fluorescent tubes.

While watching the interview with Leon, Bryant turns to Deckard and gives him the story in more detail, explaining that there was an escape from the Off-world colonies a few weeks ago: originally, *six* Replicants (in the novel, eight)—three male and three female—slaughtered 23 crew and passengers on a shuttle.[18] Three nights ago, he goes on, they then tried to break into the Tyrell Corporation, where *two* of them (according to the Final Cut; *one* in the Theatrical Release) were electrocuted attempting to break in, while the remaining four vanished. Bryant says that he suspected they might try to infiltrate the corporation disguised as employees and so he sent Holden there to run Voigt-Kampff tests on all the new workers, whereupon Holden—unfortunately—located Kowalski.

Leon, he explains, whose "incept" data now appears on the monitor before them, was an ammunition loader capable of lifting four hundred pounds. (In the Workprint version, Deckard's voiceover explains, as Gaff is flying him to Tyrell's office, that Leon's pain sensors had been jacked up so high that the only way you could hurt him was to kill him) Note that Leon's "birth" date reads 10 April, 2017.

Deckard says that he doesn't understand why the Replicants would risk coming back to earth, and what they would want out of the Tyrell Corporation, but Bryant points out that that is precisely what he is hiring Deckard to find out. (In Dick's novel, by the way, the androids have come down from Mars to earth merely to escape the boredom and ennui of the red planet. Hampton Fancher's screenplay adds the ingenious plot motivation—at Ridley Scott's prodding[19]—of the Replicants coming down to earth specifically to have their four year life spans extended by Tyrell).

Bryant then introduces Roy Batty as his data comes on-screen, and explains to Deckard that he is a combat model and most likely the leader of the four escaped Replicants. His birth date, take note, is given as January 8, 2016.

Zhora's data then flashes up onto the monitor (her birth date is 12 June, 2016). Bryant explains that she was trained to be part of an Off-world murder squad, and that she is both beauty *and* beast (according to Deckard's voiceover in the Workprint as he is sifting through a dossier on his way to the Tyrell Corporation, Zhora was originally a "pleasure model" that was redesigned as part of a homicide squad).

Finally, the data for Pris then flashes onscreen (birth date: 14 February, 2016 [Valentine's Day, as Paul Sammon points out]). Bryant explains that she is a "basic pleasure model" and is a standard item for military elites in the outer colonies.

The Nexus 6 generation, Bryant then explains to Deckard, was designed to mimic humans in every way except in terms of the complexity of their emotions (as we have seen). However, the Tyrell designers feared that after a few years they might actually develop their own emotions, and so built into them the fail-safe device of limiting their life spans to four years (whether this was done only for the Nexus 6 generation, however, is unclear; in Dick's novel, *all* the androids have four year life spans, but if this were true for the film, then Bryant would hardly need to point this out to a seasoned Blade Runner like Deckard).

Bryant then says that he wants Deckard first to travel to the Tyrell Corporation, where there is a Nexus 6 Replicant—named Rachael—that he wants Deckard to put through the Voigt-Kampff test to make sure that such a test still works for detecting the Replicants of this dangerous new generation that is increasingly becoming more and more like humans in almost every respect.

Deckard then posits the key question: what if the machine doesn't work? To which Bryant gives no response and looks vaguely uncomfortable (which implies that in that case, they would have to create yet another new test to catch up with The Tyrell Corporation's handiwork).

Now, I have been drawing the reader's attention to the birth dates of the four Nexus 6 Replicants for a reason. Note that the dates for Zhora, Pris and Leon each correspond to three of the four seasons of the year—summer, winter and spring in their cases—but that Roy Batty's birth date, January 8, also puts him in winter along with Pris (February 14), whereas the attentive viewer might have expected him to have a date that would correspond to Fall.

If *Blade Runner* was a Modernist work of art, that might have been the case, but in the post-metaphysical age, there is always a "slippage" in which signifiers do not *quite* align with archaic structures from the mythical or metaphysical ages. Joyce divides *Finnegans Wake* into *precisely* four parts that correspond to Vico's Four World Ages, just as T.S. Eliot does something similar with his *Four Quartets*. However, in a Thomas Pynchon novel— *Gravity's Rainbow*, for instance—the structures do not *quite* correspond to the four signs of the zodiac associated with the sun's equinoctial and solstitial points of the Piscean Age.

This misalignment of the seasonal structures of the birth dates of the four escaped Replicants—just as they kill *23* and not *24* people on the shuttle that they have escaped from—indicates that there is a sort of Lacanian "gap" in the film's symbolic order, for that misalignment in which the four birth dates *just* miss corresponding to the four seasons suggests the possibility for new meanings to emerge. Signifying structures in the post-metaphysical age do not precisely map on to the archaic structures of the metaphysical age because this is an age in which all traditional meaning systems are in full disintegration. There always exists the possibility that new meanings will escape through the cleft in the misalignment, and in *Blade Runner*, all metaphysical structures which, at first glance, appear to correspond to metaphysical age structures will, by the film's conclusion, deconstruct themselves and shift off the scale into the Red Zone of Derridean "undecidables."

In a 1996 text by Jean Baudrillard entitled *To Do Away with Freedom*, he insists that we now live in the "fractal" rather than the "fatal" age, for it is an age in which truth, like the cosmological image of the universe itself, no longer fits into simply one or two or three dimensions, but has rather become "interstitial." As he writes, "just as a fractal object is no longer in a complete dimension but in 1.2 or 2.3 dimensions, so an event is no longer true or false but oscillates between 1.2 or 2.3 octaves of truth."[20]

Thus, as Deckard will eventually discover, Replicants too are not simply human or not-human, but rather 1.2 or 2.3 degrees "human." He will find that they cannot be classified so easily and therefore exterminated by a Blade Runner with a free conscience.

The film does, though, make use of *some* mythical and metaphysical age structures: the fact that there are *four* Replicants who have precisely *four year* life spans—the sum total of their temporal allotment adding up to 16 years collectively, therefore comprising a set of four 4's—would suggest that they constitute a sort of Jungian mandala of four functions. (In the ancient world, this would have corresponded to the four cardinal directions and / or the four signs of the zodiac assigned to each age of that slippage known as the "precession of the equinoxes." But then all signifiers of the mythical and metaphysical ages came in either sets of four or three, or else constituted dyads).

Considered thusly, the group of four Replicants before us does constitute one of the film's bivalent structures that I had mentioned in the previous chapter: in this case, two women and two men. It is therefore not an accident that *one* female Replicant and *one* male Replicant were killed attempting to break in to the Tyrell Corporation. That leaves a perfect metaphysical mandala for Deckard to deal with.

There are also a couple of Jungian 3:1 ratios, for three of the surviving Replicants are all associated with violence and combat—Leon, Roy and Zhora (hence the archetypal sphere of Mars)—while there is only *one* pleasure model (associated, therefore, with the sphere of Venus, as signified by assigning Pris's birth date to Valentine's Day). It is also the case that whereas Leon, Zhora and Pris display, through the course of the narrative, little to no empathy toward humans, it is only Roy who shows any capacity at all for empathy when, at the end of the film, he saves Deckard's life. (And here it hardly needs to be remarked that Pris's "friendly" attitude toward J.F. Sebastian is entirely faked).

On the Jungian model, Rachael would thus constitute the "fifth" or "transcendent function," the axial pivot directly in the center of the mandala, for she differs from all the other four in that her life span was specifically designed by Tyrell to be indeterminate.[21] She is also *quite* capable of love and empathy (she first saves Deckard's life when she shoots Leon in the head; *then* falls in love with him).

The film, however, though it borrows, recycles and uses structures from both the mythical and metaphysical ages, is nevertheless thoroughly *post*-metaphysical in its sensibilities.

For just as Rachael's life span is undetermined, so the viewer—along with Deckard himself—will discover that nothing in the universe of Blade Runner is metaphysically certain. Codes—genetic, linguistic, technological, etc.—are inscribed, reinscribed and uninscribed, but none are fixed and all are subject to revision or dismantling.

Thus, this final mission that Bryant assigns to his former Blade Runner Rick Deckard will turn out to be not just any ordinary mission for him, but one that changes the entire ontological

structure of his life as it erases all his previously expected certainties and replaces them with a series of *un*-certainties.

(15:39 – 22:39)
Rachael

The Workprint voiceover tells us that Gaff picked Deckard up the next morning in order to fly him, via police spinner, to the Tyrell Corporation headquarters where he will perform the Voigt-Kampff test on one of the Nexus 6 Replicants. Deckard, in this version, sifts through a dossier on the Replicants while on his way there—much like Willard does in various scenes of *Apocalypse Now*—but in the Final Cut this data has been removed, since most of it was already conveyed in the previous scene's video conference with Bryant. Instead, with the voiceover from *both* the Workprint and the Theatrical Cuts now absent— and both are *very* different narratives—the present scene follows a horizontal vector—whereas previous scenes have had vectors of either ascent or descent—that leads from the police precinct straight across, through the pink and azure wash of the early morning sunlight, to the Tyrell skyscrapers. In this version, we are not privy to Deckard's thoughts, and so we don't know what he's thinking as Gaff pilots the spinner down to the roof of the Tyrell building.

Once inside the main office of the Tyrell skyscraper, Deckard waits as he watches a synthetic owl fly across, left to right, from one perch to another located on the other side of the room. At that moment, the Nexus 6 Replicant named Rachael steps into the Gothically cavernous office, while behind her, Ridley Scott frames her together with a bronze or gold statue of an eagle. Rachael asks Deckard whether he likes their owl, and he inquires whether it's artificial, to which she responds, "Of course it is," as she strides forward, high heels echoing across the surface of a polished black marble floor. In the wider framed shot of her that follows, there is an eagle statue on a long pedestal located to either side of the entrance behind her. (The eagle was, of course, in Greek myth, associated with Zeus, for we are here at the top of a mechanized equivalent of Mount Olympus).

Deckard then surmises that the owl must be expensive and Rachael confirms that it is *very* expensive, then introduces herself to Deckard, who reciprocates.

Rachael comments that it seems the police think their work at the Tyrell Corporation is not beneficial to the public, to which Deckard responds by saying that Replicants are just like any other machine in that they are either a benefit or a hazard, and that if they happen to be a benefit, then it's not his problem.

The two are standing before a long oak or perhaps mahogany table upon which a bonsai tree has been placed symmetrically at either end. Beyond the desk, Tyrell's office faces the rising sun, which is captured behind the skyscraper's twin building and framed in a long rectangular window as a glowing red orb, freshly risen.

Deckard is wearing his long brown trenchcoat and Rachael is clad in an elegant black dress that looks as if it were somehow made out of ebony. She wants to ask him a personal question, to which he assents, and then proceeds to ask Deckard whether he has ever retired a human being by mistake. He tells her that he hasn't, but she insists that for someone in his position, that must be a risk.

However, before he can answer, Eldon Tyrell steps into the room and asks Deckard about the Voigt-Kampff test, wondering if the test that he is about to perform is to be an empathy test tracking the blush response, capillary dilation and dilation of the pupils.

As Deckard rises from his seated position at the table, Scott frames the shot so that Tyrell's office resembles an Egyptian pharaoh's domicile, with a series of granite or limestone pillars—their capitals inverted to the floor—supporting a ceiling that is lost in shadow, with the burning red disc of the sun, hanging in a copper sky, framed in the long, rectangular window behind them.

Deckard informs Tyrell of what he must certainly already know: that the test is called "Voigt-Kampff" for short. Rachael then introduces Deckard to Tyrell, and the viewer wonders that the two have never met, since Deckard has spent his entire career hunting down and destroying Tyrell's creations.

Tyrell presently insists that the test be demonstrated immediately and when Deckard asks who might be his test subject, Tyrell says that he wants him to try it out on a human being first. When Deckard asks what the point of that would be, Tyrell raises his right hand and insists that Deckard "indulge" him by testing it on Rachael.

Deckard agrees, then insists that the room is too bright for the test, so Tyrell, who appears to have power even over the sun itself, disappears into a murky corner and hits a switch that causes a dimming veil to descend down across the window, plunging the room into a blue-gold pool of squirming shadows and orange morning sunlight.

As Deckard proceeds to unpack his Voigt-Kampff device, Rachael, seated across from him, asks if she can smoke and he says that it won't affect the test. The mechanical arm then slides into place and Deckard watches as it captures one of Rachael's eyes on its video monitor.

Deckard then informs her that he will now ask a series of questions and that she should just answer them as simply as she can.

The questions are taken almost verbatim from Dick's novel,[22] although in the novel, *all* of the questions feature an animal in them in one way or another, since the point of the test in the book is to trace for a person's empathic responses to the near extinction of all animal life on earth. Whereas humans would be sentimental and nostalgic about their disappearance, Replicants would be simply indifferent to them.

Hence, the first question he asks regarding someone giving to Rachael a catskin wallet for her birthday: Rachael says she wouldn't accept it.

Deckard then moves on to the next question and hypothesizes that her little boy shows her his butterfly collection with the killing jar, to which she responds by saying that she would take him to the doctor.

Deckard then tells her to imagine that while watching television, she notices a wasp crawling on her arm, but she cuts him off and says that she would kill it immediately.

He then suggests that while reading a magazine, she comes across a nude photo of a girl, but Rachael interrupts and asks whether the question is designed to test whether she is a lesbian or a Replicant, to which Deckard impatiently tells her to just answer the question. He then goes on to say that she shows the photo to her husband who likes it so much, he hangs it on his bedroom wall, to which Rachael responds by saying that she wouldn't let him as she would be "enough for him." (In the book, this particular question points out that the girl in the photo is specifically lying on a *bearskin* rug; hence the novel's ubiquitous animal motif).

Finally, after over 100 questions, Deckard concludes by telling her that she is watching a stage play with a banquet in which the entrée consists of boiled dog, but Rachael fails, for some reason, to respond to the question, and so Deckard shuts off his machine.

Tyrell then asks Rachael to step out for a few moments, and Deckard tells him that his test has revealed her to be, indeed, a Replicant. Tyrell points out, however—proud of the handiwork that has gone into his difficult-to-detect Nexus 6 generation—that it took Deckard over 100 questions to figure that out, whereas Deckard admits that it normally only takes him about 20 or 30.

Deckard then puzzles over the fact that Rachael herself seems not to know that she is artificial, while Tyrell suggests that she is beginning to suspect the truth. Deckard still wonders how it is possible that "it" cannot know what "it" is, and Tyrell replies by saying that it is all a matter of commerce: "more human than human" is the Tyrell motto. Tyrell then elaborates by saying that he began to recognize in the Replicants an obsession with their emotions, and he decided that by "gifting" them with an artificial past he could create a "pillow" or a "cushion" for their emotions and consequently control them better.

"You're talking about memories?" Deckard realizes, astonished at the Tyrell Corporation's latest advances in human synthetic replication.

Tyrell is, of course, The Great Father, whose metaphysical-age pedigree extends back to the time of the Old Testament and Homer. In this respect, he has displaced The Great Mother, whose origins go all the way back to the first ivory-carved Venus figurines of the Upper Paleolithic. And whereas The Great Mother was all body—with incised vulva prominently emphasized—carrying no identifiable facial features at all, Tyrell is primarily just a walking cranium[23] (highlighted by his huge trifocal glasses and dark blue suit which causes his body to disappear into the shadows of his office), for he has appropriated the metaphysical vulva from the Great Mother and used it as the power to give birth via the Logos, the Word that he makes Flesh daily inside his genetic vitrines from out of which his Replicants are spawned.

From this point of view, Rachael can be identified with Athena—whose animal signifier was the owl—for she is Tyrell's mindborn child, thought up and conceived within the vault of his skull and grown inside of his laboratory. The other Nexus 6 Replicants are also his mindborn children, for just as Zeus, in appropriating the metaphysical vulva from the Great Mother gave birth to Athena, goddess of wisdom and the arts, when Prometheus chopped into his head with an axe, so Adam, likewise, gave birth to Eve from the vaginal cleft in his side from whence Great Father Yahweh borrowed one of his ribs. (This vaginal cleft becomes, of course, the spear wound in the side of Christ from whence the boon of Eternal Grace flows into the world like wine).

In the Workprint version of the film, this scene contains a shot of a synthetic dog with glowing artificial eyes like those of the owl (and also Rachael's), which is notable in that dogs in mythology are almost universally associated with the Underworld: Cerberus is the three-headed hound that guards the entrance to Hades, for instance, while Yama, the Lord of the Dead in Vedic myth, has a pair of hounds. For though, in Tyrell's office with its pair of bronze eagles—sacred to Zeus—we are at the top of a mechanized Olympus, the scene is not semiotically "pure" but contains a mixed hybrid of both Underworld and celestial signifiers, for Rachael will, during the course of the narrative, become Deckard's Eurydice that he must redeem from captivity in Tyrell's Plutonian corporation-as-apparatus of capture. (Though Deckard does not know this yet, the Voigt-Kampff test nevertheless becomes a mythic equivalent of Orpheus singing in the underworld so beautifully that he is allowed to leave it with the shade of his beloved provided that he does not look at her as he is exiting. In this case, Deckard should not look too far into Rachael's "virtual" existence as a synthetic human if he wishes to sustain a romantic relationship with her).

Tyrell thus plays the role of both Pluto *and* Zeus, just as Rachael is in the double role of both Athena *and* Eurydice. (Deckard is in the role of both Orpheus *and* Shiva, the great destroyer of forms).

The way in which the sun is framed in the rectangular window, and the apparent command which Tyrell has over it when he dims its luminosity, is interesting, too, because it suggests that Tyrell has opened up a world horizon in Heideggerian fashion between "world" and "earth,"[24] in which bioengineered entities are unconcealed as synthetic truth events. That is to say, Tyrell's entities are spawned from the interiorized vulva of his brain within a world horizon that he has opened up between earth and sky, mortals and divinities (Heidegger's famous "fourfold" that his aesthetic theory on the work of art setting forth a world in opposition to an earthly resistance evolved into)[25] in which Tyrell plays the divinity—i.e. the God of Biomechanics—who manufactures his "mortal" creations in the horizonal "cleft" that he has opened up between earth and sky.

That Tyrell's office faces the rising sun invites, too, a certain comparison with the Egyptian tradition, beginning with the mortuary chapels of their Fourth Dynasty pyramids, of orienting their temples to greet the rising sun, which they imagined as emerging from the vulva of the cow goddess Hathor each morning. Indeed, in one tradition, the falcon god Horus, whose right eye becomes the sun, is thought to be her own child (later he was assigned to Isis as his mother, who assumed most of Hathor's iconography and cult apparatus).

The rising sun is indicative of the birth of consciousness and is appropriate for the scene, since Rachael is Tyrell's newborn masterpiece, fresh out of the "replicant vat," as Ridley Scott once put it,[26] created with an indeterminate life span and with an unexpected depth of emotions and memories. She is "new" to the world and her life is just dawning.

Neither is Rachael "hollow" inside like the other Replicants, as Deckard is astonished to discover in this scene, but is rather capable of both love and empathy, as he will find out. And once he finds that out, he will do everything he can to steal this Eurydice from the realm of Hades and escape with her from its labyrinth to the sun-washed greenery of the expansive countryside.

Kowalski's Apartment

The Workprint version of this scene is much longer, featuring a shot of Deckard searching the bedroom of Kowalski's grimy apartment, looking under the mattress, etc., while Gaff, meanwhile, is shown entering the bathroom, urinating in the sink, and then finding the piece of paper that he uses to create his little origami stick man. Also, when both Gaff and Deckard leave, the viewer finds out that Kowalski has been hiding in the bathroom all along, for he emerges from it, looking perplexed as he picks up Gaff's tiny stick man and contemplates it for a moment.

In the Final Cut, Deckard gets Kowalski's address from listening to the taped interview with Holden inside the police spinner in which Gaff is flying him from Tyrell's office. After Gaff and Deckard have landed, there follows an exterior shot of the two standing outside in the rain—it is now night—looking up at the Yukon Hotel where Kowalski was staying. The hotel proprietor is then shown opening the door to let them inside Kowalski's apartment, whose name he announces before walking away, while Gaff and Deckard step into a small sparsely furnished apartment with paint peeling from its walls, the whole room striped in shadows from Venetian blinds, a soft vanilla-colored light flooding in through them.

Gaff enters first, leaning on his walking stick—he apparently suffers from a limp of some sort—while Deckard immediately goes into the darkened bathroom in which a fluorescent light buzzes like a wayward fly as it comes on. Gaff, meanwhile, is shown already making his stick figure outside the bathroom door, while Deckard is then shown leaning over the bathtub where a tiny pool of silver luminescence dances as he reaches for what appears to be a fish scale from the dirt left in the tub by some recent bather. Deckard examines the scale on the tip of his finger a moment before letting it slide into a small plastic bag which he seals up.

As he emerges from the bathroom, Gaff has just finished with his latest origami "Replicant," the figure of a stick man with an erect phallus, which he places on top of the bureau, again beside another ashtray.

An exterior street shot then follows, showing an apprehensive Leon lurking below the building.

Deckard is then shown opening the bureau's top drawer, which contains only a newspaper, which he pulls back to look beneath, finding nothing, before moving on to the second drawer, which is full of neatly folded clothes. Beneath these clothes, he finds what appears to be a stack of family photographs.

The stick figure that Gaff makes in this scene is interesting because Gaff, we learn, suffers from a limp, and the motif of the "limping hero" is a very well known and widespread motif in ancient mythology that connotes impotence and sterility.[27] So the figure's erect phallus is an interesting compensatory image to Gaff's limp, as though he were somehow "completing" himself by means of an artificial supplement. (The man with an erect phallus is also a very old motif, going clear back to the Shaft of the Dead Man at Lascaux, which shows a shaman with an erect phallus who has just eviscerated a buffalo with his spear.[28] There also exists a stamp seal from Mohenjo-daro that possibly depicts the god Shiva sitting in yogic posture with an erect phallus,[29] so there is a long history of association between the depiction of an ithyphallic figure with the entry into altered states of consciousness. Hermes, in ancient Greece, was originally signified by pillars known as "herms" which often featured the god with an erection, for Hermes is the god who guides dead souls into the Underworld, just as Deckard, following his instincts—which Gaff caricaturizes here in a comment on Deckard's "hard on" for the case—is finding his way through the labyrinth of the Hadean Cityscape that he is trapped in).

That the fish scale turns out, later on, to be a snake scale is not an accident, either, since snakes were creatures in ancient myth with a chthonic valency (Hermes, recall, had a caduceus, or staff with a pair of entwined serpents on the end of it). The snake sheds its skin, which is why, in the Gilgamesh Epic, after the plant of eternal youth is stolen from Gilgamesh and eaten by a snake, the snake was thought in the ancient world to have the power of casting off death by eternal rejuvenation. Once again, the film's theme of the quest for immortality—since the quest of the Replicants to find their Maker and win more life from him echoes that of Gilgamesh's quest to find Utnapishtim, the Flood survivor from a previous World Age, in order to find a way to extend *his* mortality, of which, following the death of his best friend Enkidu, he is terrified of losing.[30] The Replicants' quest for more life, then, is metaphoric of the more universally human quest for immortality, found only by means of the various world religions (or, in India, yoga; in China, alchemy, etc.) which enable one to realize one's true Self as an immortal soul.

The artificial memories which Tyrell has implanted within the Nexus 6 generation of Replicants—and which, in Leon's case, find their mediatic sign carrier in the form of these faked photographs—are the temporal counter sign to the Platonic Idea of immortality (also one of Kant's Ideas of the Reason which the Understanding can never penetrate). As Proust demonstrated in his epic novel, *Remembrance of Things Past* (known, by another translation, as *In Search of Lost Time*), it is precisely the awareness of the passage of time via the flow of memory which causes the human being to become anxious about his or her own mortality and to find some means of accessing a submedial space, as it were, that lies somewhere beyond this temporal flow of memories.

The film's central irony, then, is that Tyrell, specifically by implanting artificial memories in his Nexus 6 Replicants as a means for, as he put it, of "controlling them" better, has most likely actually *caused* them to become anxious about their own mortality and therefore drives them to become so desperate about finding a way out of their mortal confinement. It is precisely the awareness of time's passage through the flow of one's own memories that leads the human being to suspect the possibility of an immortal soul that lies somewhere *beneath* or *beyond* this temporal flow.

These Replicants are a very different generation of Replicants from anything that Deckard has ever encountered before, for they are not quite as hollow inside as his Voigt-Kampff tests have led him, over the years, to believe of the average Replicant.

This Nexus 6 batch is something altogether new, a bioengineering singularity of an Evental nature in which Alain Badiou's "empty set" from a previous status quo situation has now been ruptured and filled by an anomaly indicating the occurrence of a true Event: the Replicant with a soul.[31]

(25:05 – 30:20)
Chew's Eye Works

There now follows an exterior street shot in which the rumbling of some industrial machine comes over the soundtrack. Inside a VidPhon booth, the viewer is introduced to the leader of the Replicants, known as Roy Batty, whose hand is presently cramping up on him as his genetically engineered body—with its planned obsolescence—begins its dying process. Batty clenches his fist and mutters, "Time...enough," then hears Leon tapping on the phone booth glass from outside. Stepping out of the booth, he meets Leon, who is standing with a desultory look on his face and Batty asks him if he has managed to retrieve his "precious photos," to which Leon shakes his head and informs Batty that someone was inside his apartment. Batty asks if it was a man, and Leon nods, but then Batty specifies, "*Police*...man?" But Leon doesn't answer and Roy turns away, disgusted, while Leon follows him up the sidewalk past a pillar lit by stacks of blue neon tubing.

As they walk past a series of Syd Mead-designed parking meters with red and blue lights on them (and which, according to Mead, will electrocute anyone who tampers with them), the camera then tracks left into the middle of the street, down which a group of Chinamen are riding bicycles past a central pillar with white script written upon it in Chinese, at the base of which huddle two people trying to keep warm in front of a makeshift fire. (One has the sense here of fragments of signifiers from all the world's great metaphysical systems that have been "deworlded" and ground up inside this Hadean cosmopolis).

The next shot watches Roy and Leon enter a green-fluorescent lit establishment with Chinese writing on the left of its entrance and on the right, scrolling upwards are the words "Eye Works." (The voiceover narration from the Workprint tells us that this is the location of "Hannibal Chew's Eye Works," a man who does contract work for the Tyrell Corporation).

Inside the Eye Works, Chew is just pulling a synthetic eye with a pink stalk attached to it from a small yellow and white plastic container using a pair of tongs. Speaking Chinese to the eye, he places it at the base of a microscope and proceeds to examine it. The room is filled with frosty blue light, and a camera shot at floor level then shows the entrance sliding open, and the feet of Roy and Leon entering and walking along a creaking wooden pathway.

Another shot reveals Chew seated at his work table from behind, and shows that the heavy coat he is wearing is hooked up to a series of tubes—presumably a heating system to keep him warm—while Roy Batty's hand grabs the tubes in a bunch and yanks on them to get Chew's attention. (Chew has the appearance of some kind of underworld creature from out of Milton's Hell, with serpents growing out of his back and multiple eyes on stalks sprouting forth from his body).

Startled, Chew turns around to see them and then speaks into his microphone for his assistant to come help him, but the microphone doesn't seem to be working and Chew looks panicked.

Roy then steps forward and quotes a few lines from William Blake's poem, "America: a Prophecy," although the lines have been deliberately *mis*-quoted by screenwriter David Peoples, for Roy says: "Fiery the angels fell; deep thunder rode around their shores, burning with the fires of Orc."

60

The lines from Blake's original poem, however, read as follows:

Fiery the Angels rose, & and as they rose deep thunder roll'd
Around their shores: indignant burning with the fires of Orc
(Am 11: 13-14)

The "Angels" in Blake's poem refer to the thirteen original states of America, which are "rising" in their revolt against their British colonizers. However, by changing their "rise" to a "fall," Peoples manages to evoke Milton's *Paradise Lost*, which opens with the angels who have revolted against God falling into the pit of Hell. Batty is therefore suggesting that he and the other Nexus 6 Replicants are like the fallen angels who have gone to war against their maker, in this case, Tyrell, the God of Biomechanics.

Chew speaks angrily to Roy and tells him that it is illegal for them to be in his establishment. He then notices Leon reaching his hand into a freezing blue liquid containing a reservoir of Chew's manufactured eyes, but Leon, instead of feeling anything, merely pulls his hand out and looks curiously at the glowing fluid on it. Chew now realizes the depths of the trouble that he's in.

He turns back to Roy, who is smiling, as Roy tells him he has questions regarding "morphology, longevity, incept dates." Chew insists that he doesn't know anything about such complicated stuff—although not before Leon rips open the back of his coat, leaving Chew exposed to the cold like a creature without its exoskeleton. Chew then tells Roy that he only designs eyes, and that he most likely designed Roy's, since he is Nexus 6.

To which Roy says: "Chew, if only you could see what I've seen with your eyes."

Roy insists, however, on answers to his questions, and Chew says that he doesn't know anything that could help him and that

61

only Tyrell could possibly know these things, as Tyrell was the one who designed his brain. Roy then surmises aloud that Tyrell must not be an easy man to *see*, and then seats himself, in the frigid blue air, across from Chew as Leon stands behind him and places one of Chew's synthetic eyes on his left shoulder.

Chew then informs Roy that the man he needs to see to get into the Tyrell Corporation is one J.F. Sebastian, and Roy, with a gleam in his eye, presently leans back in his seat and demands to know just *where* they would find this "J.F. Sebastian" character.

Though the filmmakers don't show it, Chew's fate in this scene is likely sealed, as the original screenplay involved a later scene in which Deckard discovers Chew's body in his lab and somebody accidentally knocks it over and shatters it into pieces. (The scene was not filmed due to budgetary considerations).[32]

Chew is here in the role of the Greek mythical figure known as Argus Panoptes (or "All-seeing"), who was born from the soil and had eyes all over his body. Zeus tasked him with guarding the cow Io, but he was slain by Hermes, while Hera took his eyes and placed them in the tail feathers of her peacock. That he was born from the soil—according to one account—suggests that his birth was parthenogenetic, meaning that Gaia herself simply gave birth to him without insemination by a male. In *Blade Runner*, however, Chew is a miniaturized and modified version of Father Science, the one who has taken the biogenetic powers of the Great Mother away from her and interiorized her metaphysical vulva as the power to create life from the utterance of the Word (or, in the case of science, the power of its mathematical equations). (The actor, James Hong, who played Chew, says that he spoke Chinese to his eyes as though they were his "little children."[33]

But Chew, unlike Tyrell, can only give birth to eyes, as though they were emerging from all over his body—whereas Tyrell designs brains. Chew's eyes are a three-dimensional response, then, to the two-dimensional eye that appears on the Blade Runner's

Voigt-Kampff machine. It is primarily by means of the test subject's eye that the Blade Runner is enabled to discern a fake human being from a real one, and so there is a certain irony in that it is an eye designed by Chew that the Blade Runner is looking out for in his tests. Chew's synthetic eyes are a dead giveaway.

The Panoptic, or All-seeing, Eye in the Western metaphysical tradition, furthermore, was the Eye of God, which is found in Renaissance painting and iconography—especially in the designs of the mystic Jacob Boehme. In the world of *Blade Runner*, however, the metaphysical Eye has been appropriated, mechanized and imitated by Father Science who has transformed it into a technological object. The huge, staring eye at the beginning of the film announces its thematic presence as the All-Seeing Eye of a completely urbanized society over which the authorities—both the corporations and the police—are always watching. Anywhere you go in such a society, the Eye follows, but it is an electronic eye.

Chew's synthetic eyes, which are three-dimensional and grown in vats, are not allowed in this digitized unconcealing of Being-as-being-watched (which also gives us a clue to how the Replicants are created in a sort of piecemeal manner, rather than being completely grown through the embryogenic unfolding of more cells from fewer cells. The Replicants are somehow "pieced" together: the eyes from Chew, the brain from Tyrell, etc. etc. The analogues from the metaphysical vulva of Father Science are never quite as good—or as convincing—as the children of the Great Mother, who grew Argus from her own soils).

So Chew here is slain—just as Argus is slain by Hermes—by beings with a chthonic or "underworld" valency, who are using his eyes to make their way into the kingdom of Zeus at the top of a mechanized Mount Olympus.

(30:21 – 36:19)
Rachael and Deckard

The next shot features Deckard driving home at night through a tunnel paved by glazed ceramic tiles shining with moist green light (the so-called 2nd Street Tunnel in Angeles), listening, once again, to Holden's interview with Leon as he drives through the rain. There follows a shot of his car pulling up to the front gate of his skyscraper apartment, while a xenon spotlight slowly rotates towards the viewer's gaze, drowning the scene—and along with it, the buildings—in white light. Another shot then shows Deckard's car pulling in through the gate, its windshield covered with tiny pools of origami-like rain.

As he steps into the elevator, the computer asks him for his voiceprint identification and floor number, which he gives as the 97th floor. (That he lives so high up indicates a transcendent attitude "above" the Replicants, whose Nexus 6 complications will slowly bring him down to the earth). By the time the elevator reaches floor 97 and the door slides open, Deckard senses that there is someone else with him on the elevator, hiding in the corner shadows and so he pulls his gun out, but then recognizes Rachael and puts it away. She follows him out of the elevator into a hallway with walls covered by Frank Lloyd Wright-style panels coated with soft vanilla light. Behind him, Rachael insists that she wanted to see him, so she waited for him to get home. Deckard, flustered, digs his electronic key card out of his coat pocket and drops it, while Rachael, dressed in a heavy, fur-lined dark blue coat, picks it up and gives it to him. He asks her, irritated, why he would need *her* help as he slides the key card into its slot to open his front door.

Rachael says she doesn't know why Tyrell told Deckard what he did, but Deckard only tells her to go back and talk to *him* about it before slamming the door in her face just as she is saying that Tyrell refused to see her. But after a pause, Deckard relents and opens the door, walking away from it and leaving it ajar for her to enter.

Inside his cave-like apartment, a rectangular window with Venetian blinds that looks across into another apartment emits a flood of xenon light as Deckard asks Rachael if she would like a drink. As he steps across the room to the bar, an energy-efficient light that resembles a stove-light springs into being by itself, casting a smoky shaft on the glass of liquor that he is pouring for himself, since Rachael seems uninterested in alcohol. She asks him whether he really thinks she's a Replicant, but he doesn't answer as he drinks from his shot glass and crosses the room to seat himself in a softly cushioned chair in the murky corner. "Look," she says, handing him a photograph—which he does not bother reaching for—"it's me with my mother."

Deckard gives forth a skeptical, "Yeah?" and asks her to remember when she was six and she snuck into a basement with her brother to play doctor, who showed her his, but when it came time for her, she chickened out and ran. He asks her whether she ever told *that* memory to anyone. (In the Workprint version, Deckard's voiceover informs us that, after his first meeting with Rachael in Tyrell's office, Tyrell proceeded to show him a scan of all of Rachael's memories, which is how Deckard knows the contents of her mind).

Then he asks her if she remembers the spider with the orange body and green legs that lived outside of her window, and how she watched it build its web all summer long. Then one day, its egg hatched and—Rachael finishes the memory for him—"a hundred baby spiders came out and they ate her."

Deckard explains that what she thinks are her own memories are actually implants, memories from Tyrell's niece that have been transferred artificially to her own mind. But this upsets Rachael—for her emotions are real enough—and she begins to cry, so Deckard backpedals and insists that he was only making a bad joke. He tells her to go home and rises, apologizing, not knowing how to handle emotions from a Replicant, which takes him completely by surprise. He stands awkwardly a moment, uncertain what to do, then insists that he will get her a drink as he walks over to his tiny, cramped kitchen, where the lights, sensing his presence, come on all by themselves. He digs a glass out of the sink that is full of dirty dishes and begins to wash it, but notices that Rachael is on her way out of the apartment.

As he sets the tumbler full of whisky down on a desk that is crowded with office materials, stationery and an open briefcase perched precariously atop a stack of books, he notices that Rachael has dropped the photograph of what she insisted depicted her and her mother. As he examines the photograph of Rachael—actually Tyrell's niece—and her mother, the photograph comes to life for a moment and tree shadows begin to squirm across the front porch as the distant sounds of children at play can be heard on the soundtrack.

Deckard is then shown examining Leon's photographs as he drinks his whisky, sifting through them and pausing at one that appears to be of Roy Batty with his white hair seated at a table—perhaps in Leon's apartment—arm raised pensively to prop up his head (again implying an introspective interiority that should not be there).

He sets the photos aside, then steps out onto the rainy balcony with his liquor, gazing down over the edge into the luminous, glowing canyon below formed by the skyscrapers stacked in rows along his street. A police spinner with a pink halo of light around it rushes off toward some distant crime far below. Indeed, the buildings are so densely packed that it appears as though the city were the only thing that existed, and Deckard lived inside an underground cavern with no sky, only buildings stacked vertically storey upon storey.

Deckard is so moody in this scene because his encounter with Rachael and her emotions is the first time in his career as a killer of Replicants that he has had to face one with real emotions and depths that appear to be every bit as genuine as human subjectivity. Thus far, he has been able to live with himself as an exterminator of Replicants because he has been taught that Replicants, unlike human beings, have no interiority whatsoever. They are not "subjects" in the properly metaphysical sense, that is, human beings capable of acts of free will. Replicants, because they do not have emotions and are therefore incapable of things like love and compassion, have no true free will, since their acts are limited to the fight or flight responses of the reptilian brain stem. Killing Replicants has been no more complicated for him than killing reptiles or insects.

But Rachael is different—and here, the viewer surmises the delight that Tyrell must have taken in upsetting Deckard's world as an exterminator of his creations with Rachael, his "more human than human" masterpiece—for her emotions are indeed real and she is, therefore, *not* hollow inside.

At the start of the film, in the sequence involving Holden's interview with Leon, a binary opposition had been set up that goes something like this:

Human	Replicant
Genuine	Synthetic
Subjectivity	Hollowness
Emotions	Fight or flight responses

But the earliest beginnings of the erosion of this binarity comes with the Voigt-Kampff test that Deckard performed on Rachael in Tyrell's office, deliberately mirroring and echoing Holden's Voigt-Kampff test with Leon that almost ended in his death. It takes Deckard over 100 questions to determine Rachael's synthetic nature, for her emotions appear to be genuine, and so the Voigt-Kampff questions-as-probes had to be sent farther and farther downward into the murky depths of Rachael's interiority before it found the wall of the proscenium supporting the illusion of interiority.

In the present scene in which Deckard is confronted with the unsettling possibility that Rachael's emotions are real—even if her memories are not—this binarity is beginning to erode further as Rachael-as-Replicant begins to shift out of the simple category of "Replicant" and moves to the left, into an indeterminate Between that looks something like this:

Human	Replicant
Genuine	Synthetic

Rachael-as-Undecidable

Subjectivity	Hollowness
Emotions	Fight or flight responses

The binarity, in other words, is beginning to deconstruct itself and is no longer so neat and clean, just as the truths of the post-metaphysical age (i.e. after World War II) are no longer anchored in Transcendental Signifieds that nail them firmly into place. (It is Baudrillard's truth as 1.2 or 2.3, as mentioned above). Truth has now become a hermeneutic game, as Gianni Vattimo in his book *A Farewell to Truth* points out, and the hard ontologies of traditional metaphysics have now become what Vattimo calls "soft ontologies."[34]

In the age of the hyperreal, when humans that are more human than human can be manufactured by corporations, nothing is quite so simple, neat and clean as a good old fashioned bivalent ontology—the kind that built all of the world's great religions; i.e. Good vs. Evil; sacred vs. profane; etc. etc.—since the Clearing of Being in which truths are currently unveiled is as fuzzy and low-rez as one of Gerhard Richter's late photo-paintings. It is the digitized and synthetic realm of the hyperreal that is now unconcealing its entities with higher and higher resolution, whereas the entities unconcealed in the Clearing of the arts and in metaphysics are fuzzy and going ever more and more out of focus as they slip into the interstitial spaces between dichotomies.[35]

It is an age, in *Blade Runner*, of the Darkening of Being, and the lighting up of the Hyperreal.

(36:19 – 41:30)
Pris and J.F. Sebastian

As Deckard surveys the city from his vantage point in the heights of his skyscraper dwelling, the following shot is down on the ground below, which shows the homeless Replicant Pris walking past a row of parking meters amidst vents of city steam. The Off-world colonies blimp that drifts past overhead reminds her, perhaps, of her "origins" from the world above, like the Gnostic soul spark that has fallen to earth from a realm of luminosity and otherworldly beauty.

Presently, she crosses the street after having identified J.F. Sebastian's address at the Bradbury Building—which, presumably, Roy has given her—and finds herself a place amongst the trash outside the structure, where she draws newspapers around her (as though she herself were a piece of refuse) and waits for J.F. to arrive.

After a time, his yellow and white van pulls up to the curb and he climbs out the side door, digging into his bag to retrieve the keys to his building, which he immediately drops on the rain-slick pavement (echoing Deckard dropping *his* entrance key in the previous scene). The sound startles Pris into wakefulness and she darts past J.F., knocking him down, as she skids into his van, breaking the glass in one of its windows. She pauses at the enormous pillar beside the cab and looks back at J.F., who tells her that she has forgot her bag, which she hesitantly retrieves from him.

She tells him that she is lost, but J.F. reassures her that he is harmless and then asks her what her name is. She tells him that her name is Pris and he tells her in return that he is J.F. Sebastian. Then he inquires as to where she was headed, but she claims to be homeless. J.F. pauses a moment, then begins to turn back to his building when Pris steps forward and insists that they gave each other quite a scare. J.F. agrees, and she tells him that she is hungry. He says he has food inside and invites her into his building.

Inside the building, the only light comes from xenon spotlights that shine directly down into it from the Off-world colonies blimp that floats above, for J.F.'s building is a dead one, an empty architectural shell that has been long since abandoned. Pris and J.F. enter the foyer and approach the open cage elevator, walking past a pile of discarded mannequins in a heap of dirt and debris in one of its disused corners.

As they enter the elevator and ascend through its iron shaft in the smoky and seemingly ghost-lit air, Pris asks whether he lives in the building alone and he tells her that he does, since there is no housing shortage in the area. Smoky shafts of light dart around them as they reach J.F.'s floor, which is coated with rusty pools of rain and chunks of scattered debris.

Pris insists that he must get very lonely in such a place, but he tells her that he doesn't because he "makes" his own friends, since he is a genetic designer who creates living toys. He asks whether she knows what that profession is, and she feigns ignorance as the door to his apartment creaks open and they enter the foyer.

J.F. is greeted by two of his toys, who stride forward to meet him: a Napoleon-suited Teddy Bear with a dwarf sidekick wearing a military helmet. They wish him good evening before turning around and reversing course back into the depths of the enormous apartment. One of them, the dwarf, crashes into the wall on his way, for he is defective, as J.F. is a designer of toys that sometimes do not turn out so well, just as he himself is genetically defective and crippled with a premature ageing disease known as Methuselah's Syndrome.[36]

Pris smiles at the toys, which charm her, and J.F. asks about her parents. She says that she is sort of an orphan, and when he then asks about her friends, she says that she does have some but has to find them.

J.F. then offers to take her rain-sodden things from her.

In a sense, J.F. is yet another maker of "Replicants," for whereas we have seen that Gaff reverses tiny piles of ashtray refuse into origami men and animals—and Chew was a genetic designer who specialized only in eyes—J.F. Sebastian lives in a building that is itself a gigantic midden heap from whence he reverses much larger piles of entropy into living toys. He, like Chew, is still a specialist, however—the Workprint voiceover tells us that he specializes in "hands," although there is no evidence of this in either the Theatrical Release or the Final Cut—whose creations are larger than Gaff's but yet still dwarfed by comparison with Tyrell's living masterpieces.

J.F., furthermore, has a collection of robots and automata—seen later in the film—that recapitulate the evolution of robotic design from the automata of the Medieval period which could perform simple tasks like writing or playing a musical instrument, down to Tyrell's living humans. J.F. is therefore a collector of shells, for his robots and toys are more or less dead wrecks from whence all life has departed. He himself lives in a building that is a gigantic shell, for it has no internal life and receives light only from outside in the form of the various xenon spotlights that shine down *into* it. *Nothing* radiates from J.F.'s building or his apartment: it is a dusty trash heap full of only dead things. Here, the past has died.

Pris, however, who awakens from out of a pile of garbage, enters into this midden heap as a being who is very much alive and is desirous of extending her life span even further. There is, then, a subtle way in which she comes to life for J.F. like the living statue of Galatea in the ancient myth of Pygmalion, who carved a statue of a woman so beautiful that he prayed to Aphrodite to give it life, and she did. (The mannequins which Pris and J.F. walk past in the building's ruined lobby is a subtle hint of this myth, for the mannequins remind one of statues).

But Pris's life is violent and short, and it is far too dangerous for a man with accelerated decrepitude to handle, for J.F. is slowly turning brown and brittle like an autumn leaf that is about to fall from its branch. He is a living image of death and indeed, his relationship with Pris—whom he obviously has an erotic interest in—reminds one of the Medieval motif of "Death and the Maiden," especially as captured, for instance, by Hans Baldung Grien's painting of 1517.

For, just as in Grien's painting, J.F. is death as the past, whereas Pris is both the living present with erotic potential for future life. However, her genetic code has been altered by Tyrell to include a planned obsolescence which robs her of that future, a future which, day by day, is growing dimmer and darker.

Soon, she will be reduced to the status of one of the fish-pale mannequins in the refuse pile in one of the building's forgotten corners.

She has come, then—after all—to precisely the right place to die.

Snake Scale

The next scene brings us back inside Deckard's apartment, where two huge spotlights are shining through his window, roving back and forth as the camera tracks left to a shot of Deckard seated at his piano, drunk. The Final Cut, at this point, features Deckard imagining a mysterious unicorn running through a forest. According to John Williamson in his book on the Medieval Unicorn tapestries, the unicorn was not only symbolic of Christ, but it was also associated with the so-called Holly King, who represented the waning half of the year—from summer solstice to winter solstice—while the Oak King represented the waxing half. As the days grow shorter, and the darkness of the night encroaches, the leaves begin falling from the trees until the branches are bare, and indeed, the Replicants in the film—with the exception of Rachael—are leaves that have begun to turn brown. The light of their consciousness is running out, growing shorter by the day.[37]

Deckard is sitting at his piano with a collection of photographs of his dead ancestors splayed out across the sheet music in front of him. (The Workprint features a photograph of him standing and smiling with his wife Iran on the steps of some front porch that echoes Rachael's photograph of her with her "mother"). Deckard now reaches for one of Leon's photographs that he has pinned up, and grabs his bottle of liquor to cross the room toward his computer. Leon's photo, however, forms an interesting contrast to Deckard's collection of ancestral photographs, since Deckard's dead ancestors point to the river of time, a long river which—assuming Deckard *isn't* a Replicant—flows way, way back into his genetic past. Indeed, as the French contemporary artist Christian Boltanski has remarked, each one of us is surrounded by a halo of dead ancestors[38] which forms our genetic lineage and grounds us in an "authentic" biotemporal flow which the Replicants, by contrast, do not have. Note that Leon's photographs are only of *other* Replicants, not an ancestral archive of dead relatives. They are pure productions of an ahistorical society that produces simulacra without a past, and in which History is dead and no longer exists. The Replicants, in other words, do not have an ontological Underworld to which they can refer back to. They are synchronically anchored only in the *now* and thus find themselves completely deworlded.

Deckard presently climbs over his couch to his so-called "Esper" machine, which was originally conceived by the filmmakers to be his own in-house extension of the central police computer.[39] He pours himself another drink while the computer brings up a low-rez version of Leon's photograph covered now by a blue grid and white cross-hairs. The photograph—possibly taken by Leon himself—appears to show Roy Batty sitting at a kitchen table, arm raised to his head pensively. Deckard tells the computer to execute a series of maneuvers, one of which leads him to a sequined dress hanging on a door that makes him wonder about the scale that he had found in Leon's bathtub. (It is as though with the woman, who is supposed to be the Replicant Zhora— but is in fact a different actress, not Joanna Cassidy—there is a subtle evocation of the myth of the Animal Woman who marries a shaman in Native American mythology and takes off her animal skin—often that of a fox—and hangs it up near the door at night. Zhora is a post-historic evocation of the ancient Snake Woman).

The computer then scans behind a doorway to reveal a woman taking a nap on a bed, and when Deckard zooms in on her, there is a snake tattoo on her left cheek. He tells the computer to give him a hard copy showing an extremely grainy image of her face. Deckard then examines the scale in its plastic baggy and wonders about it for a moment.

In the Workprint version, the next scene shows Deckard sitting back at the Noodle Bar, and as he is eating, he glances at the man's fish on the plate beside him and carefully picks one of its scales off, much to the indignant man's warnings to keep away from his food.

In the Final Cut, however, the next scene shows Deckard wandering through an area of the city known as Animoid Row, where synthetic animals are routinely manufactured. He comes to the stand of a Cambodian merchant and asks her whether the scale in the plastic baggy might be that of a fish, but when the woman puts it under her electron microscope and finds a serial number inscribed on it, she recognizes that it is a snake and tells him to try the snake-maker, Abdul Ben Hassan.

Deckard next finds himself in the shop of Abdul Ben Hassan, who at first tries to give him trouble, but when Deckard grabs his tie and yanks him forward, Hassan tells him that the snake was indeed manufactured by him, for he illegally puts the same serial number on each one of his snakes. But Abdul Ben Hassan refers him to the establishment of Taffy Lewis, where he will most likely find the snake dancer.

The snake, of course, reiterates the movie's central theme of Time and the flow of Temporality, for the snake sheds its skin just as the moon does on a monthly basis. The snake in ancient myth has the power to defeat death by shedding its skin, which is one reason why it is associated with the iconography of the medical profession. It represents the power to throw off death.

Deckard is now following the path of the serpent to its lair.

(47:38 - 59:26)
Zhora

Deckard now finds himself at a crowded bar known as the Snake Pit, a seedy establishment operated by Taffey Lewis. The bar is noisy—it reminds one of a Parisian Folies-Bergere out of an Impressionist painting—and Deckard finds Lewis seated at the main counter. He asks the proprietor whether he has ever bought snakes from the Egyptian and Lewis tells him, with a smirk, "all the time," but then when Deckard shows him the photograph of Zhora, Lewis tells him to "buzz off, pal." Deckard then threatens to investigate all his licenses and so Lewis orders him a drink to mollify him.

As Deckard drinks, he sifts through the Replicants' photographs, and then when he finds the one which Rachael had dropped on his apartment floor—supposedly of her and her mother—he decides to call Rachael and invite her down to the bar for a drink. He goes to a "Vid-Phon" on the wall and types in her number, and when Rachael appears onscreen, he tells her that he's had people walk out on him before but not when he was being so charming. He then says that he is in a bar in the Fourth Sector and invites her to come down for a drink, but she declines, saying that it's not her kind of place. When Deckard offers to take her somewhere else, she hangs up on him.

Deckard then returns to the bar for another drink while an impresario announces the next act, "Miss Salome and the Snake," and promises the audience that she will "take the pleasures from the serpent." (Originally, the filmmakers had decided to insert a larger sequence at this point with Zhora doing her snake dance, but were unable to film due to budgetary considerations). Zhora's snake dance is, of course, a contemporary updating of the ancient Minoan Snake Priestesses, for the serpent is associated, as we have said, not only with Time, but with Death, as well. The serpent is civilization's dying and reviving male god, while the Great Mother—here reduced to a dancer in a seedy club—represents the eternal energies which animate her serpent lover, whose life is always brutal and short.

Zhora, interestingly, embodies the energies of both Venus and Mars, for she was originally designed as a pleasure model which was then reprogrammed to become part of a homicide squad. She is, therefore, a combination of the twin sisters at the dawn of civilization in Sumer—Inanna, goddess of the World Above—and Ereshkigal, mistress of the World Below. She is both Great Mother *and* Amazon synthesized together.[40]

Deckard then waits back in the hallway of the dressing rooms pretending to read a newspaper when Zhora, snake draped around her shoulders, passes him. He asks to speak with her, pretending that he is from the American Federation of Variety Artists and follows her back inside her dressing room, where he then tells her that he's actually from the Committee on Moral Abuses. He explains that there have been reports of management taking liberties with some of the artists but she says she knows nothing about it and does not feel exploited.

As Zhora undresses in order to take a shower, Deckard tells her that she would be surprised what a man would go through to get a glimpse of a beautiful body, but she tells him that she would not.

While she is showering, Deckard finds a couple of sequined dresses that match the one in the photograph hanging in her dressing room. Zhora is then shown blow-drying her hair, and as she is getting dressed, Deckard asks whether her snake is real, to which she tells him she couldn't afford a real snake just by making a living in a seedy place like the Snake Pit.

She asks him whether, in case she *does* feel exploited, who she would go to in order to file a report about it and he tells her, "Me." She tells him that he's a dedicated man, then throws her towel at him and orders her to dry her.

But before he gets a chance, she turns and hits him, twice, hard enough to knock backwards onto the ground. Then she proceeds to try and strangle him with his tie, but another dancer walks in at just that moment, causing Zhora to flee.

She runs out into the noisy, smoke filled, overcrowded streets, as Deckard follows her, gun drawn. He pushes his way through the crowds, many of them carrying luminescent blue and white umbrellas, but Zhora momentarily disappears into a traffic jam. Deckard spots her on the other side of one of the buses and when she notices him, she panics. But then he loses her again and stands looking around while a Trafficator buzzes the electronic phrases of "cross now" and "don't cross" over and over again.

Zhora tries desperately to blend into the anonymity of the crowd, but it is impossible because her motions are so frantic that she stands out and Deckard soon spots her again. She jumps across a car as Deckard yells for people to move out of his way, raises his gun and fires at her. Her right shoulder explodes in a crimson eruption that sends her tumbling through a series of store windows with neon signs burning inside them. He shoots her in the back once more and this time she crashes through another glass pane out on to the sidewalk, where she lies splayed on her stomach, bleeding mortally.

A group of policemen turn her over onto her back, and gradually the sound of her beating heart fades and then stops. Deckard then identifies himself to the police as a Blade Runner.

Meanwhile, Leon has been watching the whole thing from across the street.

Zhora is in the ontological status of what Giorgio Agamben termed "bare naked life."[41] That is to say, she has no metaphysical immune system to protect her and she has found herself on a world island in which the juridical order has been entirely withdrawn from her, leaving her exposed. She had attempted to disguise this "nakedness" by disappearing into the anonymity of a show dancer, but the city's immune system, using Deckard as its white blood cell, targeted her through clever detective work and eliminated her from the system.

Zhora, along with the other three Replicants who escaped to earth with her, are all ontologically dewordled. They literally have no world to call "home" which can function as a protective shell around them, and so each one, with no metaphysical structure in place to support them, is naked and exposed. They are floating signifiers drifting across a global ecumene that has no place to situate them.

They have, furthermore, no ancestral bio-pool to connect them to a temporal matrix that would help function to give them a history and thereby a "world" of some sort.

They are "worldless"[42] beings on a planet in which the city itself has become a vast and inescapable world island. Fake human beings have no place in a world island in which the city has completely replaced nature and most animal and plant life.

And a worldless being, like an astronaut floating free from his space station in orbit around the earth, is completely exposed, metaphysically, ontologically and immunologically. The four Replicants on earth are about as vulnerable as such an astronaut in space and now find themselves in an increasingly desperate situation, for they have no Temporal Matrix behind them or in front of them, and no Spatial containers within which to embed themselves.

They are spaceless, timeless, ahistorical beings.

But Tyrell, their Maker, has made the mistake of giving them memories and therefore interior subjective consciousness, a consciousness which feels that it *should* have these things, since the emotions of Nexus 6 Replicants are as indistinguishable from those of real humans as are their bodies. The Voigt-Kampff test can barely detect them anymore, and almost *didn't* work on Rachael. So the police department of 2019 Los Angeles is finding itself in a situation in which it cannot keep up with the technological advances of the big transnational corporations which are rapidly outmaneuvering it

(59:32 – 62:77)
Leon and Deckard

In the Workprint version, Rachael, too, is shown having watched the execution of Zhora from across the street and when Deckard spots her, the two of them are seen walking side by side, making their way through the crowded, rainy street to the neon-illuminated liquor kiosk. But in the Final Cut, it is only Deckard who now arrives at the tiny, steaming light-soaked kiosk to order a glass of liquor when Gaff taps him (once again) on the shoulder with his cane, which Deckard grabs angrily. This shot mirrors the opening encounter of Gaff with Deckard at the Noodle Bar, and once again, Gaff tells him, "Bryant." Deckard nods and grabs his bottle of liquor as the side door of Bryant's spinner, which has just landed, slides up and the captain steps out into the rain, telling Deckard that he looks almost as bad as the skin job that he left out on the sidewalk.

Deckard tells him that he's going home for the night, but Bryant informs him that he still has four more Replicants to retire. Deckard then corrects him and says that there are only three, but Bryant then explains that Rachael, the "skin-job" that he had V-K'd at the Tyrell Corporation, has escaped. Once off the premises of the Tyrell Corporation, she has lost all juridical protection and has shifted, along with the other Nexus 6 Replicants, to the status of "bare naked life," (*zoe*) that is equivalent to that of an animal which can be hunted and killed with impunity. Bryant tells him to have a drink for him, too (since he can no longer drink), then climbs into his spinner while rain glistens across it.

85

Deckard, in this version, *now* spots Rachael across the street, but she disappears once she realizes that he has seen her. He is just beginning to make his way through the crowd toward her, when he is apprehended by Leon, who is very angry at watching Deckard execute Zhora (whom, it is implied, he had a "thing for"). Leon asks him how old he is, and Deckard makes the mistake of punching him in the face (since he knows very well that Leon cannot feel pain), and Deckard tells him that he doesn't know, just as Leon slams him up against a van. Leon says that his birth date is April 10, 2017 and then asks him how long he is supposed to live, to which Deckard replies: "Four years."

Leon then swings him around and slams him into the side of another truck and when Deckard pulls out his gun, Leon bats it from his hand, and tells him that he now has longer to live than Deckard does as he picks him up and smashes him into the windshield of a parked car. Leon tells him that there's nothing worse than having an itch that can't be scratched, to which Deckard agrees, as Leon then stands him up, slaps him twice in the face and tells him to wake up, "it's time to die."

But just as Leon is about to use the first two fingers of his hand to poke out Deckard's eyes, the top of his forehead explodes with a direct shot from Rachael's gun, who stands behind him, thus saving Deckard's life.

The confrontation between Leon and Deckard is interesting since when Leon makes the remark that it is painful to live in fear, the viewer realizes that the entire scene is a miniature version—and foreshadowing—of Deckard's later encounter with Roy, which will simply be a much longer version of the same encounter (with the asymmetric difference that Roy saves Deckard at the last moment).

And the irony that Leon intends to kill Deckard by poking out both of his eyes not only foreshadows how Roy Batty later kills Eldon Tyrell by doing precisely the same thing, it also loops back to Dave Holden's original detection of Leon as a Replicant precisely by means of the Voigt-Kampff test which uses a close up video scan of the eye—designed to search for one of *Chew's* eyes—to ferret him out.

If, as the Medieval truism went, the eyes are the window to the soul, in *Blade Runner*, they are also the gateway to the realm of the dead, for all Replicants are found and detected precisely by use of an electronic eye that *sees through* one of Chew's genetically designed eyes just as though it were made of stained glass (thereby reversing the truism, since, in that case, the eye of the Replicant becomes the window to the *absence* of the soul, detecting only a miniature hollow cavern that is made out of matter, but void of *spirit*).

The Eye of God found at the top of the pyramid on the back of the dollar bill is a signifier left over from the Renaissance, as in Pontormo's 1525 painting *Supper at Emmaus* in which the eye inside the triangle above the head of the seated Christ is indicative of the inescapable power of the All-Seeing Holy Spirit. Likewise, with the famous Medieval portraits of Christ in which the incarnate god's eyes are rendered in such a manner that no matter which way one looks at the painting, one cannot escape the gaze of the Redeemer, who watches over, and sees all.

But in the age of Foucault's disciplinary societies, the eye was panopticized to indicate that the individual was watched, no longer by God, but by the rise of the new post-sovereign institutions—hospitals, clinics, prisons—that were emerging to track him via documentation and paper work no matter where in the system he found himself to be located. The rise of the disciplinary institution, which subjectivized the individual by tracking him,[43] created the all-seeing society that was then, in the biopolitical age, transferred to the panoptical gaze of the electronic eye of what Zygmunt Bauman calls "liquid modernity." [44]

For as Rilke put it, in his poem Archaic Torso of Apollo, "there is no place that does not see you. / You must change your life."[45]

It is the tracing out of a line of flight that escapes this modern electronic panoptified eye that Deckard, once his life begins to change, must now find a way to escape. He must move *out* of the arena where he can be seen and tracked no matter where he finds himself, and escape from the Hadean underworld to the countryside, beyond the gaze of *all* eyes, artificial or otherwise.

Rachael and Deckard (Redux)

The Workprint version begins this next sequence inside Deckard's apartment with him washing his face in the bathroom sink, while Rachael seats herself on a hard-backed chair, legs loosely opened as she watches him from across the room. The scene is much longer, and Deckard, still bent over the sink, notices Rachael with her legs apart just enough to reveal the white of her panties—an echo of Scott's shot of Ripley's white panties as she climbs into her space suit in *Alien*—and once again, this is not a gratuitous shot and should have been left in the film, for it highlights the movie's central thematic concern of birth from the metaphysical vulva. The shot of Rachael's panties is an image of the metaphysical vulva on the plane of the Real, whereas Tyrell has already appropriated the female birth-giving powers and interiorized them into his psyche on the level of the symbolic, with the power of the Word—that is to say, the right mathematical equations—to generate life artificially in a laboratory.

The shot also functions as a "hook" for Deckard that incites his erotic interest in a Replicant, feelings which are overcoming him for the first time in his career as an exterminator of artificial human beings.

In the Final Cut, the scene is shorter and begins with Deckard nursing a glass of liquor in an alcove of his kitchen while Rachael, in the corner, is drowned in luminous white from one of the exterior searchlights that are forever crawling through Deckard's apartment. He asks her if she has the shakes and he tells her that he always gets them after such tense encounters. He says that shakes are just a part of the business, but Rachael tells him that she *is* the business.

It is at this point in the Final Cut that Deckard retires to the bathroom and removes his gun and shirt in order to wash his face in the sink while Rachael steps forward to look at him, fascinated. She pauses at the threshold to the bathroom and asks him what would happen if she went north and disappeared: would he follow her? Drying his hair with a blue wash cloth, he tells her that *he* wouldn't—since he owes her one—but someone else would.

Deckard grabs his bottle of liquor and strides across the apartment into the bedroom area where exterior spotlights are soaking it with blinding luminescence, and Rachael asks him about the files on her which contain her incept dates and longevity information. She wants to know if Deckard ever saw them, but he tells her they're classified, and when she insists that he's a policeman and could look at them if he wanted to, he tells her, evasively, that he never saw them.

As he pours himself another drink and sits down on his bed, Rachael asks him whether he himself ever took the Voigt-Kampff test, but when she doesn't hear a reply, she enters his bedroom to find him passed out on the bed, precariously balancing a shot glass full of liquor on his stomach.

She then wanders over to the piano, where she plucks one of the photographs of his dead ancestors from in front of the sheet music, as though in contemplation of what it would be like to be descended from a line of authentic human beings. While Deckard sleeps, she removes her jacket and begins to play Chopin's *Thirteenth Nocturne*, a sound which draws Deckard forth out of his sleep. Rachael undoes her hair, pulling down the curls and carefully arranging them to frame her pale, lovely face while Deckard stumbles from his nap and crosses the room to seat himself at the piano beside her. He tells her that he dreamt music, and she begins to play again, commenting that she wasn't sure if she could play since she has memories of taking lessons but doesn't know whether the memories are hers or Tyrell's niece's.

Deckard tells her that she plays beautifully, then leans forward to kiss her cheek softly, but when he attempts to kiss her again, she retreats and tries to flee (once more) from the apartment. Deckard stops her at the door, slamming it shut with his fist as he then shoves her back against a window striped with cream-colored venetian blinds. He kisses her again, on the mouth this time, and then tells her to reciprocate. When she hesitates, he orders her to say, "kiss me," and when she does so, he kisses her on the mouth, fiercely.

The Workprint version contains a somewhat longer, more erotically explicit version of this same scene which makes it clear that sex follows, and once again, I think the filmmakers should have played the stronger erotic material, since it leaves no doubt in the viewer's mind about Deckard having sex with a Replicant that he is falling in love with for the first time.

In the film, there is some question about Rachael's longevity since, in the Theatrical Release voiceover that Deckard speaks at the film's conclusion, he implies that not only does Rachael not have a four year lifespan but that her longevity might be completely indeterminate. This raises the possibility that she might even be cleverly designed by Tyrell to be immortal, whereas Deckard is decidedly mortal (even if he is a Replicant, since he would have only a four year lifespan). If so, then Deckard's having intercourse with an immortal casts him in the role of those ancient and unfortunate mythic figures—Tithonus, for instance, the mortal who married the goddess Eos, the dawn, whom Zeus granted immortal life but not biological immortality and so, as he aged and withered, Eos locked him away—of mortals who have love affairs with gods and goddesses.

But the function of the scene is that Deckard now realizes that certain Replicants exist who are *not* hollow inside, but are capable of depths and therefore have interiority and subjectivity. Whether Rachael has the kinds of "abysses of freedom" within her that Schelling spoke of as so ennobling and essential to the human subject remains unknown,[46] but Deckard realizes that he is capable of loving her and that is enough for him. However, this Fall into the *Abgrund* of primordial emotions scrambles his carefully arranged metaphysical binarity in which one is either a human being or a Replicant, for Rachael is slipping into that Baudrillardian "interstitial space" of truth in which she is not quite either / or. She is 1.2 or 2.3 degrees Replicant / human and is therefore an undecidable.

From Rachael's point of view, she is envious of Deckard's bio-genetic temporal matrix of dead ancestors, since she has none, and having sex with him is the only possible way of inserting her-self into that biotemporal gene pool. This raises the question of whether a Replicant could have a child since, if Rachael ever did become pregnant, she would be the First Ancestor of her own biogenetic line of descendants, a kind of Eve of a special class of Replicants.

Either way, their union evokes the ancient myths of mor-tals having affairs with the immortal gods and goddesses, affairs which almost always betoken disaster for the mortal in one way or another.

(In the ancient Sumerian myth of Inanna and Shukal-letuda, for instance, the latter is a mortal whose gardens are failing, but one day, when he plants a special sacred tree his garden flourishes. The goddess Inanna happens to be crossing the sky one afternoon and decides to take refuge beneath the tree for a nap. When Shukalletuda sees her beauty, he takes advantage and ravishes her, but when she awakens to find out that a mortal has defiled her, she is enraged and sends three plagues on the city that Shukalletuda has chosen to hide in. The ending of the story is not known, but clearly, dalliance with a goddess is a dangerous thing, to say the least).[47]

(72:42 – 79:74)
Pris, Sebastian and Roy

Next, there is a brief shot inserted of the luminous skyscraper canyons on one wall of which a giant video geisha girl is seen putting a contraceptive pill into her mouth (according to the film's production designers), an interesting irony in light of the semiotics of the previous scene. One thing the overcrowded world city does *not* need is more people, but it is precisely *into* the human genetic flow that Rachael wishes to insert herself.

The next shot takes place inside J.F. Sebastian's apartment, where Pris is seen airbrushing a raccoon kabuki mask onto her face. A cuckoo clock goes off in the corner as a signifier of the early automata that eventually led to the biogenetics of creating artificial humans, and a shot follows of J.F. taking a nap in his work chair, surrounded by his various creations: mannequins, statues, dolls, a toy unicorn, all of them unmoving and still with the exception of the trembling Napoleon-suited dwarf with the Pinocchio nose. Pris does a cartwheel in the background as she creeps up on J.F. and leans over to sniff him, while the dwarf looks nervous as Pris then moves to peer through a viewfinder of some sort that spills a soft yellow light upon her doll-like face.

At this point, J.F. suddenly wakes up and asks her what she's doing and she tells him that she was "just peeking." Then she asks him how she looks and J.F. tells her she "looks better," but Pris says, "Just better?" and he admits that she does indeed look beautiful. (She actually now resembles one of J.F.'s own mechanical dolls).

There follows a shot of Roy Batty striding confidently through the building's denuded corridor, searchlights spawning pools of light and squirming shadows around him.

Back inside, Pris is asking J.F. how old he is, and when he tells her that he is only 25 years old, she asks him what his problem is, to which he replies that he has Methusaleh's Syndrome, a disease that accelerates his ageing process. He tells her that he is still on earth because he couldn't pass the medical exam that would've allowed him to migrate to the Off-world colonies.

Looking past J.F., Pris greets Roy as he enters and says, "Gosh, you've got a lot of nice toys here."

Pris introduces J.F. to Roy as the friend she was telling him about, her savior, J.F. Sebastian. Roy tells him that he likes a man that stays put and then asks him whether he lives in the building by himself, to which J.F. assents.

As Roy leans forward to kiss Pris, J.F., obviously uncomfortable, abruptly stands and asks them whether they would like some breakfast, saying that he was just about to make some anyway. While he is gone, Roy informs Pris that there are only two of them now, and Pris replies that they are stupid and they will die. But Roy looks at her with a clever smile, and tells her that they won't.

In the next shot, Roy wanders through the corridors of J.F.'s vast apartment, admiring the various dolls and automata. As J.F. brings them their breakfast, Pris sits in a chair with one leg tucked up underneath her, holding half a doll and dangling it by its hair. Roy then spots a chessboard and reaches forward to move a piece, but J.F. stops him and tells him that it is the wrong move, for in that case the knight would then take the queen.

As Roy seats himself before the luminous chessboard—all the pieces of which are birds of various species—he asks why J.F. is staring at them and J.F. tells them that they're so different and so perfect, then asks them what generation they are. Roy climbs onto the chair behind Pris and informs J.F. that they are Nexus 6, and J.F. excitedly tells them that there is some of him in them since he does genetic design work for the Tyrell Corporation.

J.F. asks for a demonstration of their abilities but Roy insists that they aren't computers, but rather physically inclined. Pris climbs to her feet and paraphrases Descartes: "I think, Sebastian, therefore I am," and Roy then tells her to go ahead and show J.F. why. Pris then performs a backwards cartwheel and reaches her hand into a beaker full of boiling eggs and pulls one out and tosses it to J.F. who cannot hold it in his hands and drops it.

Roy then tells J.F. that he and they have a lot in common: accelerated decrepitude. J.F. then says that he knows very little about biomechanics, but Roy, suddenly fierce, grabs J.F. and insists that if he and Pris don't find help soon, then Pris hasn't got long to live.

Roy then glances at the chessboard and asks J.F. whether his opponent is any good. J.F. says that he has only beaten Dr. Tyrell once in chess and that he is a genius, for he designed both Roy and Pris. Roy suggests that possibly Dr. Tyrell could help them and J.F. volunteers that he would be happy to mention it to him. But Roy insists that it would be better if he talked to him in person.

As J.F., intimidated now by Roy, finds himself moving backwards between Pris's legs, who sits on the pool table behind him, Roy says that he understands Tyrell would be a hard man to get to see. J.F. tells him that he is *very* hard to see, and Roy asks him whether he will help them. J.F. insists that there's nothing he can do, and Pris tells him that they need him, as he is their best and only friend.

Roy then picks up a pair of artificial eyes encased in glass containers and holds them up to his own eyes, creating an effect that is both comical and eerie at the same time as he tells J.F. that he and Pris are so happy that J.F. has found them.

J.F. laughs and Pris tells him that she doesn't think there's another human being in the whole world who would help them. She then kisses his cheek, but he looks decidedly nervous as he walks away and Pris and Roy exchange knowing glances with one another.

Whereas the previous scene in which Deckard and Rachael make love points to the future and has connotations of life, pulsing blood and the possibility for the generation of new human / Replicant hybrids using the old-fashioned means of sexual reproduction, the present scene inside J.F. Sebastian's apartment, with its clutter of automata, lifeless mannequins and discarded objects, is concerned strictly with the past, for J.F., as remarked, is a collector of dead things and a maker of defective toys. His realm is a world of brittle fallen leaves and decayed and discarded objects, and it foreshadows the fates that both Pris and Roy—as merely more elaborate toys—have in store for them, for they will soon be added to his collection of dead, dry, dusty things.

When Pris tosses the hard-boiled egg at J.F. and he drops it, it is because he himself is an egg that has been dropped and is now cracked and defective. The egg is symbolic of the future and neither J.F., nor Pris, nor Roy have one.[48] They are all cracked eggs that will never bring forth life again (in contrast to Rachael, who may indeed come equipped with eggs capable of fertilization that will plug her into the biotemporal matrix of the line of dead ancestors).

Pris has already made herself up to resemble one of J.F.'s lifeless dolls, for she will soon be added to his collection as a permanent acquisition of his museum of automata.

And when Roy picks up the pair of artificial eyes and holds them up to make J.F. laugh, the scene foreshadows the fate of Dr. Tyrell, the God of Biomechanics whom Roy will kill precisely by poking out both of his eyes.

The cuckoo clock that announces the time, as well as the array of various clocks hanging on the wall, underscore the fact that for Pris, Roy and J.F., time is running out. They are trapped, like J.F., who was unable to migrate to the heavens—traditionally the realm of the immortal gods in ancient myth—on the earthly plane of mortality from which they cannot escape.

And as for the collection of various species of birds that comprise the chess pieces, as Jean Gebser has pointed out, the traditional symbol for the "soul's death pole" is that of the bird, by contrast with its life pole, which is that of flowing water. The Egyptian ba was a bird with a human head capable of leaving the tomb at night to travel through the astral plane and return in the morning. [49]

For whereas Zhora was associated with the snake—itself an image of temporal flow—Pris and Roy are associated with birds (note the dove that leaves Roy's hands at the film's conclusion). They are death-birds, however, which will soon depart from their mortal coils.

(79:74 – 86:55)
Tyrell

In the next shot, an exterior elevator is making its way up to the top of the Tyrell skyscraper, as Roy and J.F. Sebastian attempt to infiltrate the corporation. There follows a shot of Tyrell's synthetic owl (owls, incidentally, are universally associated with the underworld in ancient myth) which is followed in turn by a shot of Tyrell lying in his bed trading stocks. His room is golden-orange, for it is lit only by candle light and draped in white linen curtains that surround him like a shroud. On the nightstand beside him, there is a statue of a bronze eagle located to the right of his bed. (The Workprint version features a shot of him drinking a glass of milk, which is significant since Tyrell is the Great Father who has stolen the powers of the metaphysical vulva from the Great Mother and is drawing nourishment from the many-breasted Artemis of Ephesus as a sort of fluid which inspires his creations).

The voice of a female computer interrupts to let him know that a Mr. J.F. Sebastian wishes entry to his quarters, and Tyrell, speaking into the intercom of the private elevator, asks J.F.: "at this hour?" He then asks what he can do for him and J.F., standing beside Roy in the gloomy elevator, gives him the coordinates for a chess move: Queen to Bishop 6. Tyrell mutters "nonsense" and then climbs out of his bed and puts on his slippers, then crosses the gold-shadowy room to his chessboard, where he turns on an electric light to peer at it. Tyrell mutters that "knight takes Queen" and then asks J.F. what's on his mind.

In the elevator Roy then whispers, "Bishop to King 7, checkmate," which J.F. then repeats aloud to Tyrell who tells him that he'd better come up and discuss the situation.

The elevator then continues its ascent to the top of Tyrell's skyscraper.

There follows a shot of Tyrell's synthetic owl, and then Tyrell's bedroom door opens and J.F. steps in with Roy walking behind him. J.F. tells Tyrell apologetically that he brought a friend with him, and as Tyrell is adjusting his plush white bathrobe, he tells Roy that he is surprised that he didn't come to see him sooner.

Roy, striding ominously forward, tells Tyrell that it's not an easy thing to meet his maker, and Tyrell then asks what it is he can do for him. Roy ponders whether the Maker can repair what he makes and Tyrell then asks him whether he would like to be modified.

Roy tells J.F. to stay where he's at, and then steps forward to confront Tyrell, explaining to him that he had in mind something a little more radical.

When Tyrell asks him what seems to be the problem, Roy tells him flatly: "Death."

Tyrell backs away as Roy approaches him, saying that this is something out of his jurisdiction. In the Final Cut, Roy then says, eyes gleaming with tiny copper discs: "I want more life, Father," but both the Workprint and the original theatrical release have him saying, "I want more life, *fucker*." The latter line is much more effective due to the irony it suggests in that Roy was made precisely not by fucking at all, but by the power of the Logos as symbolic vulva in the mind of the Great Father.

Tyrell then explains to Roy that to make an alteration in the evolution of a life system is always fatal. He points out that the genetic coding sequence, once established, cannot be revised. When Roy asks why not, Tyrell explains that by the second day of incubation, any cells that have undergone reversion mutations

102

give rise to revertant colonies like rats leaving a sinking ship. Then the ship sinks.

When Roy asks him about EMS recombination, Tyrell says that they've already tried it and the process created a lethal virus that killed the patient before he left the table.

Roy then wonders about the possibility of a repressive protein that would block the operating cells; to which Tyrell responds that though it wouldn't obstruct replication it *would* give rise to an error in replication, which would end up creating a virus again.

Tyrell then says that all of this is academic, for Roy was made as well as Tyrell could make him. And when Roy points out, "But not to last," Tyrell counters by saying that the light that burns twice as bright burns only half as long, and Roy has burned so very, very brightly.

Tyrell then tells him that he is the Prodigal Son and quite a prize, and that he should revel in his time. Roy admits that he has done some very questionable things, and when Tyrell says that he also done *extraordinary* things, Roy muses, "Nothing the God of Biomechanics wouldn't let you in heaven for."

Roy then reaches across to grab Tyrell's head with both hands in order to kiss him, but it is a Judas kiss, for Roy then begins to crush his skull with the might of both hands, punching his thumbs through Tyrell's eyes until they pop and squirt forth blood. The dead God of Biomechanics then slips from Roy's hands to fall, lifeless, to the ground.

Roy then turns and goes after J.F., who attempts to scurry out of the room, but he is unsuccessful. The next shot has Roy descending inside the elevator from the Tyrell headquarters dappled with luminous starlight shining down upon him through the elevator's glass roof.

In ancient Sumer, when one wanted to commune with the gods—who were all associated with planets and stars—one ascended the steep mud-brick staircases that were designed to carry the devotees to a small temple at the top of the ziggurat, where one could expect to meet with one or another of the Sumerian gods, who would have descended down to earth from the heavens to meet with their mortal creations. (Human beings, incidentally, were created by the god Enki for slave labor, as the gods had no wish to work the canals and plough the fields any longer, so they created humans out of riverrine mud to perform these tasks for them).

Roy's ascent up the Tyrell Corporation ziggurat-as-skyscraper is a modern retrieval of this ancient myth, only at the top of Tyrell's headquarters, he encounters not a planetary deity, but the Great Father of the metaphysical age who has appropriated the powers of the Great Mother to create life. The *imaginary* vulva of the Great Mother from the Paleolithic down to the age of the Egyptians was appropriated in the time of Homer and Yahweh as the power of the Father to bring forth life by using the *symbolic* vulva, interiorized inside of his head, to give birth simply by imagining new forms.[50] The Egyptian god Ptah, who, in the Memphite Theogony, was able to create the cosmos by pronouncing the right magic words, was already a forerunner of this appropriation.[51]

The beings created by the ancient Sumerians to do their work for them were mortal, as Gilgamesh realized when his companion Enkidu was stricken by an illness sent upon him by the goddess Inanna (later Ishtar) for making a fool out of her. When Gilgamesh, terrified at the prospect of his own mortality, then set out on a quest for the island of Dilmun in order to find the only mortal that he knew the gods had granted immortality—namely Utnapishtim, the survivor of the Great Flood—he wanted to find out whether Utnapishtim could somehow grant *him* the same kind of immortality, but he was disappointed to find out that Utnapishtim, the Water Bearer (who later became the sign of Aquarius) could not help him, for the gods, he explained to Gilgamesh, had doomed all men to mortal lives. Only he, Utnapishtim and his wife, had been granted immortal life simply because they had schemed to survive the Great Flood sent by the angry gods to wipe out all human beings.

Disappointed, and ready to return to his native city of Uruk, Utnapishtim at the last moment—and at his wife's urging—did reveal the secret location of the plant of Eternal Youth that wouldn't exactly make Gilgamesh immortal, but it would keep him physically young throughout the span of his life. As is well known, when Gilgamesh dived down beneath the springs off the coast of Dilmun and came up with the plant, he was taking a nap on his boat when a serpent crawled out of the water and ate the plant while he wasn't looking. Which is why snakes shed their skin: they have the power to cast off death, just like the moon.

In the present scene of *Blade Runner*, Roy Batty, like Gilgamesh, realizes that he is doomed to a mortal life. His maker did not make him or any of the other Nexus 6 Replicants—save possibly Rachael—to last, and so he destroys his maker by crushing his head, the very source of the metaphysical vulva that, in his role as the Great Father of the Age of Science, he used to create the Replicants in the first place. With Tyrell gone, there will be no more Replicants. (And hence, no more Off-world slave labor: it is a sort of Spartacus revolt in miniature).

(The filmmakers had originally intended for Tyrell to turn out to be a robot and for Roy to discover, on yet another floor above Tyrell's, that the original Tyrell was long since dead and cryogenically frozen in a sarcophagus at the top of the skyscraper, thus retrieving the concept of the Egyptian pyramid, or the Mesoamerican temple-tomb in which dead kings were always buried).[52]

Roy puts out Tyrell's eyes—just as Leon had been about to do to Deckard in a previous scene—because it is precisely the eyes by means of which a Replicant is differentiated from a human being. That is to say that, though to the normal human eye, one cannot tell the difference between them, the Voigt-Kampff machine was designed to specifically scan a Replicant's eyes for the correct bio-responses that become the giveaway to a hollowed out interior in which there is no subjectivity, since Replicants do not come equipped with a mammalian mid-brain, but only a neo-cortex and a reptilian fight-or-flight brain. The Voigt-Kampff is designed precisely to detect the semiotic vacancy within the Replicant where there ought to be a brain that has evolved genetically across the generations with emotional responses such as compassion, empathy and nurturing of the young. But it is precisely the mammalian mid-brain that, in a Replicant, is missing. The VK machine thus uses the Replicant's eye as the window, not to the soul precisely, but to detect the hollow interior of the semiotic vacancy where there ought to be a human subjectivity (a human, that is, which has evolved over millions of years out of an authentic reptilian-mammalian-primate gene pool). Replicants, that is to say, are synchronic and deworlded: they are not authentic products of temporal biological evolution and are thus not considered to be true subjectivities belonging on Earth, where evolution took place, but only out in space where such deworlded beings belong. They have no "home," ontologically speaking, on the terrestrial realm of earth and its evolutionary processes.

Hence, this is why Roy kills Tyrell specifically by crushing his head and putting out his eyes. The eyes and the brain were the giveaway, and the metaphysical vulva inside Tyrell's cranium the source from which the Replicants emerged. So by destroying the vulvic source which gives birth to Replicants as slaves with shortened lives, Roy is removing the possibility—as far as he is concerned, anyway—for the production of any further entities of his cursed race.

The "Retirement" of Pris

The next shot begins with Deckard's police car speeding through the L.A. tunnel with its green ceramic tiles, as the sounds of sirens announce Tyrell's murder in the so-called "12th sector." Deckard is then shown parked in the rain, while Bryant's voice informs him that the body identified with Tyrell was that of one "J.F. Sebastian," thereby confirming that Roy did indeed kill him.

In the Workprint, Deckard's voiceover tells us that he left Rachael with a gun and told her to shoot anyone that tried to enter his apartment, and that he had decided to save Tyrell's life by killing the other two Nexus 6 Replicants before they got to him. So, in the earlier version, he does not yet know of Tyrell's death.

But in the Final Cut, Bryant's voice comes over the car's intercom and gives him the address of J.F. Sebastian at the Bradbury Building and orders him to go down there, but before he can finish, he is cut off by a police spinner that floats down from above to inform Deckard that this sector is closed to ground traffic and asks him what he's doing there. Deckard replies that he's working and asks the cop what *he's* doing, to which the cop responds by telling him that he is arresting him. Deckard then gives his identification number as a Blade Runner and after the cop then looks up his data on the computer he tells Deckard that he is checked and cleared and advises him to "have a better one."

Deckard then tries to use his car's Vid-Phon to dial up J.F.'s apartment, and when Pris answers, he asks for J.F. She wants to know who is calling and he tells her that he is Eddie, an old friend of J.F.'s. She hangs up on him and Deckard mutters under his breath that that is no way to treat an old friend.

Outside the car, a group of German-speaking dwarves wearing glasses with blinking red lights attempts to pull Deckard's car apart, and so he drives onward to the address of the Bradbury Building and pulls up directly in front of it, slides open his door and steps out into the rainy night.

The shot is intercut with an image of Pris drawing a veil over her head and freezing her motion, so that now she is actually imitating one of J.F.'s automata. Bit by bit, she is slowly transforming into one of his dead and rusty toys.

Deckard is then shown stepping into the entrance of the building's foyer, with its wrought-iron balustrades and gloomy corridors and hallways illuminated only by the blue beams of restless searchlights shining down from above.

Deckard walks past a group of mannequins on his right and then hears the voice of the singing geisha girl that indicates the Off-world colonies blimp drifting past the building's rooftop, shining its spotlights down through the iron and glass architecture into the atrium below.

Deckard then cautiously ascends the iron staircase to the second floor as the searchlight beams crawl around him and the sound of running water from the rain leaking in can be heard echoing throughout the hallways. He then goes up to the third floor, gun drawn, and slowly makes his way to the apartment door of J.F. Sebastian, which is already ajar. As he enters the dusty foyer, one of J.F.'s Napoleon-suited toy dwarves passes by, then crashes, yet again, into the wall before righting itself.

Deckard enters the main living space of J.F.'s apartment, where most of his dolls, automata and mechanical humans have been gathered in a cluttered heap inside a room that is lit with a faint sunset pink-orange light. A few of the automata are still moving with stiff mechanical repetitions—one of them even laughs hysterically and continuously, as though to mock Deck-ard's search for the Replicants—and Pris is seated amongst them, frozen, her pale whitened body covered by a wedding veil.

Pris does not realize that Deckard knows exactly what she looks like, and as he spots her amongst the other dolls and toys, he reaches forward to pull away her veil, and at that moment, she springs suddenly into life and kicks him backwards across the room (echoing Zhora's attack on him that also sent him sprawl-ing backwards).

She then follows rapidly as he tumbles across the floor, doing two or three cartwheels that land her upon his shoulders, where-upon she squeezes his head between her legs as she turns him around to face her and smacks his head with both of her hands, twice. Then she inserts two fingers into his nostrils in an attempt to break his nose and drops him to the floor. She then runs back across the room to gain momentum for another cartwheel as-sault, but as she is in mid-air Deckard shoots her in the stomach with his gun and she falls tumbling to the ground, screaming. Deckard watches as she goes into some kind of inhuman frenzy, like a sprayed insect dying, then gets to his feet and shoots her a second and a third time until she stops moving.

Deckard can barely stand, but he climbs to his feet and leans against the doorway, his dirty trench coat flapping as he exam-ines his handiwork. Pris lies on the ground, motionless. She is, indeed, dead.

This sequence with the death of Pris is all about her final transformation into one of J.F.'s dead mechanical toys. There is nothing living in J.F.'s building and none but Deckard escapes it alive. It is a place that is full of relics and discarded automata from the past, as well as J.F.'s failed biomechanical experiments that Tyrell found unuseable because of their flaws. If Tyrell's skyscraper is the place of Origin from whence originate all of his living human experiments, then Sebastian's empty shell of a building is the place where they all go to die. It is a crypt for the genetic pollution discarded by Tyrell, which J.F. simply collects and gathers into a midden heap like an archaeological mound of abandoned attempts to create artificial human beings.

At one point during pre-production, the filmmakers had contemplated opening *Blade Runner* with an image of an android garbage dump on another planet, displaying a heap of discarded bodies from out of which Roy Batty, together with two other Replicants, would then be seen to crawl and make their way, as though reversing entropy.[53]

But in the final imagining of *Blade Runner*, that same termination dump evolves into the interior of J.F. Sebastian's apartment, a place where entropy is constantly and very slowly maximizing—just like J.F.'s accelerated decrepitude—and becomes the final resting place for both Pris and Roy, as though to replay the original opening scene in reverse.

If the Tyrell Corporation can be thought of as a kind of dissipative structure that functions by ejecting its entropy outside the system so that the system can run in a state that is far from equilibrium, then J.F.'s apartment building becomes its necessary supplement, where all the excreted waste of the Tyrell Corporation is ejected. It is the entropic counterpart to the maximal beauty and Pharaohnic splendor of Tyrell's office and lavish bedroom.

(93:65 – 108:67)
The Battle with Roy

The final climactic sequence of *Blade Runner* begins with a shot of Roy ascending to the third floor inside the open cage elevator. Deckard hears him coming and begins to panic, for he knows he is in trouble (Roy is the leader of the four Replicants, and his encounters with the other three have nearly killed him). Batty steps forth from the cage and begins confidently striding down the corridor outside of Sebastian's apartment as Deckard frantically searches to find a hiding place inside of it.

Deckard then waits, crouched, gun drawn as Roy discovers Pris's dead body. He gives her a final kiss and says her name, anguished. Deckard takes the opportunity to fire a shot at him down the hallway, and he hears Roy's echoing voice yelling back that it is not sporting to fire on an unarmed opponent. Roy tells him that he thought Deckard was supposed to be "the *good* man."

As Deckard stands near a crumbling wall down which streaks of rainwater are quietly slithering, he holds out his gun, tentatively, uncertain of his opponent's location. From the other side of the wall comes Roy's taunting voice and then, without warning, Roy's hand punches through the masonry of the wall and grabs Deckard's gun hand, pulling it through to the other side as he asks Deckard if he's proud of himself. He then proceeds to break one of Deckard's fingers for Zhora, and another one for Pris. Then he puts the gun back in Deckard's hand and tells him that he needs to shoot straight if he wants to get him. Deckard immediately fires through the hole but his shot only

111

scrapes Roy's ear and Roy tells him that apparently "straight" doesn't seem to be good enough for him.

Roy then tells him it's now *his* turn to set the rules and that he will give him a few seconds' head start before coming after him. As he begins his count, Deckard flees through a series of blackened dusty rooms full of derelict objects, looking desperately for a way out.

Roy takes a moment to mourn over Pris, and his tears for her indicate that he is indeed capable of love and is not at all the ordinary Replicant that Deckard had taken him for.

Deckard, meanwhile, hiding in the shadows, straightens his two fingers out and Roy can hear his screams echo through the vacant building. In return, he begins a predatory howl as he sets forth in pursuit of him.

Deckard appears to be trapped in a labyrinth of dead ends: dilapidated rooms with boarded up windows through which xenon lights rove endlessly back and forth. He then spots a massive abandoned armoire on the other side of the wall and decides to scale it.

Roy runs past the camera, singing and howling merrily, enjoying himself while Deckard, climbing the armoire, drops his gun. He has spotted a rotten hole in the ceiling through which he presently climbs, pulling himself across the slick, greasy floor to yet another empty room.

Roy's hand, meanwhile, begins cramping up on him, and he tells it "Not yet," then reaches down to pull a nail from a soggy piece of wood in the floor and thrusts it through his palm to stave off the decay of his nervous system (note that both antagonists now have severe hand injuries).

Deckard has made his way into a desolate bathroom where a tub full of murky water appears to contain something pallid and fish belly-white, possibly human, floating in it. He sits on its cracked porcelain edge for a moment to rest, but to his surprise,

Roy's head suddenly smashes its way through the black and white checkered tile of the bathroom wall. Roy informs Deckard that he'd better get it up because unless he's alive he won't be able to play the game.

Roy then pulls his head out of the masonry and steps into the bathroom, which is awash with flickering light from outside, as though a neon sign somewhere were burning itself out, and Deckard hastily proceeds to break off a metal pipe from a radiator in the corner and promptly uses it to knock Roy backwards so that he crashes into a window, glass crackling all around him. "That's the spirit!" he yells, as Deckard flees in the opposite direction through another room where pigeons have nestled in crevices throughout its broken walls and scatter as he runs through them to kick the boards out of its window. His momentum carries him to a ledge and almost causes him to fall out over it, but he regains his balance and stands overlooking a darkened canyon of buildings where almost no electricity flows.

Deckard swings out, clinging to a metal pinion and narrowly misses falling, then rights himself and begins to climb the building's rain-slickened cornice. Roy, meanwhile, has kicked his way through the rotting boards of another window, and he peers out to inform Deckard that when Deckard hit him, it really hurt. He watches Deckard begin his desperate ascent over the complex molding of the building's cornice and ponders where this little man thinks he might be going.

Deckard, almost impossibly, manages to scale the cornice and reach his hand with its two bandaged fingers over the edge of the roof, grabs onto it and pulls himself over, while lightning pops like a flashbulb and thunder rumbles all around him.

Roy, meanwhile, has taken another pathway through the building to get to the roof and Deckard, completely exhausted and worn out, climbs raggedly to his feet in a puddle of stagnant brown rainwater, shambling his way hither and thither between a series of energy-efficient wind-wheels that are illuminated, once again, by roving spotlights casting bluish-white beams over the surface of the rooftop.

Deckard is just about to make his way to a portal, when he sees Roy emerge through it and climb up onto the rooftop, so he changes his mind and turns round quickly to run the other direction and, without hesitating, jumps across to the opposite building, missing its roof and grabbing onto one of its jutting girders. He is barely able to hold on as the rain dumps down, making the iron ever more and more difficult to grasp and hold firmly. His grip is slipping.

Back on the opposite rooftop, Roy stands, pausing a moment with a white dove that he has captured, gathering himself. Then he turns and runs, making the jump across to the opposite building with ease, from whence he peers down at the hapless Blade Runner who is losing his grip. Roy tells him that it's quite an experience to live in fear, and that that's what the life of a slave is like. Living in constant fear. But just as Deckard loses his grip, Roy's lightning-quick reflexes act as he reaches out to grab Deckard's arm and lifts him up over the girder to set him down, a sodden broken mess, on top of the wet gray roof.

Roy seats himself across from him and explains to Deckard the marvelous things he's seen that other humans wouldn't believe: attack ships on fire off the shoulder of Orion; c beams glittering in the darkness near the Tanhauser Gate. Sadness and exhaustion have finally overcome him as he tells Deckard that all those moments will be lost to him now like tears in rain. He then announces that it is time for him to die and simply drops his head as his spirit departs from his body in the form of the dove that ascends above the industrial landscape and into the night sky (although in the original Theatrical Release, it was a morning-blue sky).

A police spinner presently emerges into view behind Roy and Gaff lands upon the roof, then gets out and tells Deckard that he's done a man's job. He supposes Deckard is through with his work, and Deckard, barely alive, utters the word "finished." Gaff tosses him his gun and then turns to head back for the spinner, but then pauses to tell Deckard that it's too bad she won't live, but then again, who does?

For Roy Batty, God is now dead, for he has destroyed his Maker, the God of Biomechanics. He has, in other words, drawn an "X" over the ground of Origin that gave birth to him, and so, with the goal of his quest now missing—a Gap has opened up in his symbolic universe, as Lacan would put it—he decides to transform the last moments of his life into a Homeric agon, a sort of Olympic game to reverse Entropy inside a building that is a shattered castle of Entropy where all robots come to die.

The "X" of Origin that he had sought, and found, is now replaced by an arena of Maximal Stress,[54] just as for the jaded and cosmopolitan Romans of the Last Days, the gladiatorial arenas, with all their strife, became a sort of ultimate Signified unto itself. If Spartacus was the gladiator slave who revolted, then Roy is the slave whose failed quest to extend his life reverses back into the zoological power struggles inside the hippodrome. The struggle to stay alive now becomes for him a game that gives him any kind of Meaning at all in the larger sense, and Deckard, his opponent, is forced to play the role of combatant against him.

J.F. Sebastian's apartment building is a sort of vertical labyrinth which functions perfectly for Roy as a gladiatorial arena in which all metaphysically protective laws have been suspended. Roy has transformed the building from a Zone of Maximal Entropy into a Zone of Maximal Conflict and Deckard, trapped on the inside of this zone of conflict, now finds himself on the same ontological plane as the Replicants whom he has spent his entire career hunting: no laws and no metaphysics exist to protect him.

115

He, too, now, has been reduced to the status of "bare naked life" in which absolutely anything can happen to him. Like the Nexus 6 Replicants, he can be killed with impunity inside this zone.

Roy, in overcoding the building as a maximal stress arena of combat, has captured Deckard and actually *changed* his ontological status as an immune cell of the world cosmopolis to that of a hunted animal inside of an arena that is now designed specifically for Roy's amusement.

In the age of the suspension of all Laws—political, ethical and metaphysical—the agon in the arena is all that counts, and survival the only thing that confers any sort of meaning at all.

Tyrell's corporate headquarters had been a zone governed by the laws of Eros: that is to say, of the production of living forms from out of the metaphysical vulva that he had interiorized inside the very cranium which was smashed by Roy. But once Tyrell is dead and gone, J.F. Sebastian's entropic building is reterritorialized by Roy into a zone governed by the laws of Thanatos, of fear and strife, of one self battling against another self that it is bent on destroying.

However, when Roy saves Deckard's life, a different ethic comes into play because Roy is revealed as a true Subject, capable of love (i.e. Pris) and empathy (Deckard). The feedback loop of his "I – Self" axis is ruptured by a Levinasian regard for the fate of the Other, which breaks it open to include the Other within it.[55] The zone of maximal stress is thereby immediately dismantled—together with all its amorality and zoological power struggles—and transformed via Roy's lifesaving act into a zone of cooperation. If, as Slavoj Zizek has pointed out, Levinasian ethics are the opposite of those of the biopolitical concentration camp, then Roy's lifting of Deckard from his fall is a kind of lifting of him up *out* of the biopolitical arena and into a zone of cooperation between Self + Other.

Roy thereby reveals that he is not completely amoral after all, but that an ethic of true subjectivity that has regard for the Other has been (inadvertently) built into him by Tyrell, who constructed the Nexus 6 generation specifically to have memories as a means of better controlling them. The implantation of those same memories, as remarked, were the whole reason that set the Nexus group on a quest to lengthen their life spans, for human beings are nothing if not the animal that refuses to accept zoological confinement in a biological body and reaches instead to grasp at some measure of Eternity.

The dove, of course, is an ancient symbol for the soul—witness the Christian catacombs, which were called "columbaria,"—and when it departs into the blue of the morning sky in the original Theatrical Release, it is tantamount to an awakening of consciousness from out of the long night sea journey that the film has put Deckard through. It began, with the opening shot of the Hades cityscape, with the setting sun, and I believe the filmmakers had it right when they originally ended the film with the dawning blue of the morning sky.

Deckard's consciousness has indeed been awakened and evolved regarding the Replicants which he can no longer simply hunt down and exterminate. He has unexpectedly encountered the new phenomenon of the Replicant with a true subjectivity that is just as capable of the wide range of emotions that all humans display. He can no longer hunt them with a clean conscience, especially after his life has been saved by two of them (Rachael, when she killed Leon, and now Roy). He no longer wishes to be part of the monstrous and all-engulfing cosmopolis which regards Replicants as mere machines, for the new complexities of emotion and feeling demonstrated by the Nexus 6 Replicants have dismantled his "either / or" truth system.

There are too many "undecidables" now for him to continue with the profession of being a Blade Runner.

He is, indeed, "finished."

(108:67 – 111:83)
Rescuing Rachael

In the next shot, Deckard steps out of the elevator to the 97th floor of his apartment building and crosses the balcony. His front door is ajar, so he draws his gun and says Rachael's name as he steps into his apartment that is quietly humming with electronic machinery. He enters the bedroom, where he finds a form on his bed covered by a sheet, and when he lifts the sheet Rachael is there, sleeping.

Not knowing whether she is alive or dead, he bends down to listen to her and hears her breathing. She turns over and looks up at him and he asks her if she loves him, to which she replies that she does. He then asks her if she trusts him and she says that she does trust him. He then kisses her on the mouth.

In the next shot, Deckard is shown leaving the apartment, gun drawn, making sure the coast is clear for Rachael. As she crosses the balcony, her high heels step on one of Gaff's little origami sculptures which Deckard notices and bends down to pick it up: it is a tiny tinfoil unicorn. He wonders at it for a moment and then hears Gaff's voice in his head, saying that it is too bad she won't live. He smiles to himself, then steps into the elevator with Rachael and the door closes.

At this point, the Final Cut ends and the credits come on.

Rachael has now become his Eurydice to be rescued from the Underworld of Hades. She is his beloved, a Replicant with memories and emotions, but also a different sort of being—ontologically speaking—one with an indeterminate life span that very possibly puts her into the category of an "immortal."

In the original Greek myth, Orpheus is allowed to escape Hades with his beloved Eurydice only on the condition that he not look back at her. But when, approaching the exit threshold, he trips and glances over his shoulder, she fades back into the gloom and he is condemned henceforth to a life of loneliness.

Blade Runner, however, with its post-metaphysical revisions of all the old myths, allows *this* Orpheus to leave the Hadean underworld of the city with his Eurydice intact. As he crosses the return threshold with her at the entrance to the elevator, when he looks back, his beloved does not disappear. Instead, what he finds is a tiny origami unicorn made by Gaff as his calling card to indicate that he had visited Deckard's apartment and decided to allow Rachael to live, when he could just as well have killed her.

The unicorn as a phantasmatic image thus becomes a signifier pointing the way toward escape from the realm of shades, shadows and phantoms. It does not function very well, in my opinion, as a signifier that Deckard is a Replicant—which would undermine the entire story anyway—but as a mythical signifier that a threshold guardian has allowed them to escape from their confinement in the decadent world city as Underworld which the Los Angeles of 2019 represents.

It is the Last mythical signifier that Rachael and Deckard will encounter.

Epilogue
Escape to the Countryside

In the original Theatrical Release, there is one more scene, the so-called "happy ending," which expands into a vast blue sky with drifting clouds and then cuts to a shot of Deckard and Rachael driving in a car through the fresh yellow sunlight. In the voiceover, Deckard explains that Gaff had been at the apartment and let her live: four years, he'd figured, but Deckard points out—and this is crucial—that Gaff was wrong. Deckard says that Tyrell had informed him that Rachael was special because she had no termination date and her lifespan was therefore indeterminate. He says that he didn't know how long they'd have together, but then again who does?

The shot then expands to a massive vista of open countryside, granite cliffs, green hills and mountains powdered with snow.

The commonplace assumptions about this final scene, which the filmmakers only added at the urging of studio executives, is that it is too clichéd for such a dark film, and features the hero driving away with his beloved into the sunset. But the filmmakers, in eliding the scene, have missed two points that I think are worth noting: one is that it is the first shot of full, broad daylight that occurs in the film and is consistent with Deckard's journey toward an awakening of consciousness that his contact with the Nexus 6 generation represents. His consciousness moves from darkness and an unillumined existence in the nightworld to an awakening of new possibilities never before considered by him. It is a true "dawning."[56]

The other point is that it is an image of escape from the city as underworld into a realm of greenery and countryside that functions as a semiotic double for the upper world, or the World located above the Underworld to which Deckard as Orpheus has managed to win his way. The myth of Orpheus has thereby been completely revised in this post-metaphysical work of art, and the rescue of Rachael from the labyrinthine city has allowed him to escape to an Outside, a metaphysical Outside, that was never even glimpsed in the film elsewhere.

There is a further irony in that the escape is ot *quite* so happy and simple as those who were against its inclusion—especially Ridley Scott—have supposed, since Rachael is, indeed, herself a kind of phantasmatic figure. She is a modern equivalent of Eurydice as a shade released from Hades, for she is not *quite* human, but an artificially manufactured human being with a fake set of memories and an indeterminate life span that very possibly makes her immortal.

So Deckard *has* managed to escape from the Underworld with his beloved, yet the ontological status of this beloved remains rather nervously uncertain. She *is* a kind of shade, a revenant retrieved from the World Below, and so a happy future for the two is by no means guaranteed.

I have remarked above on the unhappy fates which, in most ancient myths, have befallen mortals who have had the misfortune of erotic entanglements with immortals. Cupid and Psyche; Inanna and Shukalletuda; Venus and Adonis; Gilgamesh and Ishtar; Eos and Tithonus; the list goes on and on.

So the so-called "happy ending" is far from being semiotically pure and contains a subtle undercurrent of nervousness once it is held closely up to the magnifying glass for examination.

For these reasons, I think it should have been included in the Final Cut.

Endnotes

Introduction: On the Late Stage World City

1 Oswald Spengler, *The Decline of the West*, trans. Charles Francis Atkinson (New York: Alfred A. Knopf, 1939), 32-34.

2 Ibid., 32.

3 Boris Groys, "The City in the Age of Touristic Reproduction," *Art Power* (Cambridge, MA: MIT Press, 2008), 101ff.

4 Indeed, in one scene from the original Workprint that was cut, Gaff (played by Edward James Olmos), sitting in the conference ante-room of the police station, says to Bryant: "I spit on metaphysics!"

5 Martin Heidegger, "Building, Dwelling, Thinking," in *Poetry, Language, Thought,* trans. Albert Hofstadter. (NY: Harper Perennial: 2001) 143ff.

6 Giorgio Agamben, *Homo Sacer: Sovereign Power and Bare Life,* trans. Daniel Heller-Roazen. (Stanford University Press, 1998).

The Opening Crawl

7 Boris Groys, *Under Suspicion: A Phenomenology of Media* , trans. Carsten Strathausen (Columbia University Press, 2012), 19-31.

8 See John David Ebert, "The Cult and Culture of Celebrity," *Cultural Decay Rate: Essays on Contemporary Art, Literature and Social Disintegration* (NY: Create Space, 2015), 137ff.

9 See William Irwin Thompson, *Pacific Shift* (NY: Random House, 1986).

The Hades Cityscape

10 Paul M. Sammon, *Future Noir: The Making of Blade Runner* (NY: Harper Prism, 1996), 231.

11 See Peter Sloterdijk, "Anti-Spheres: Explorations in the Infernal Space" in *Spheres Volume 2: Globes, Macrospherology*, trans. Wieland Hoban (Los Angeles, Semiotexte: 2014), 565ff.

12 Peter Sloterdijk and Hans-Jurgen Heinrichs, *Neither Sun Nor Death*, trans. Steve Corcoran (Los Angeles, Semiotexte: 2011), 167.

13 Heidegger, Ibid., 141ff.

Holden and Kowalksi

14 For a discussion of the design of the Voigt-Kampff machine see Paul M. Sammon, ibid., 106-107.

15 Reiner Schurmann, *Broken Hegemonies*, trans. Reginald Lilly (Indiana University Press, 2003), 351ff.

16 Groys, *Art Power*, ibid. 53ff.

17 See Harlan Kennedy, "Blade Runner: Ridley Scott Interviewed ," at http://www.americancinemapapers.com/files/bladerunner.htm

Bryant

18 There was originally supposed to be a sixth Replicant named Mary (four, that is, with Rachael as the fifth), but Mary's part was cut due to budgetary reasons which is why, in the theatrical release, Bryant says that only one Replicant was fried trying to break in to the Tyrell Corporation.

19 Sammon, ibid., 53.

20 Jean Baudrillard, *To Do Away With Freedom or, How Not to Escape One's Destiny or, Fatal Against Fractal or, This World Which Thinks Us*, trans. Sylvere Lotringer (Los Angeles: Semiotext, 2015), 22.

21 See the essay "The Transcendent Function" in Joseph Campbell, ed. *The Portable Jung* (NY: Viking Penguin, 1971), 273ff.

Rachael

22 See Chapter 5 in Philip K. Dick, *Do Androids Dream of Electric Sheep?* (NY: Ballantine Del Rey, 2007), 48-50.

23 See the contrast between the body of the Great Mother and the head of the Egyptian wife of Akhenaton, Nefertiti in Camille Paglia, *Sexual Personae: Art and Decadence from Nefertiti to Emily Dickinson* (Yale University Press, 1990), 47-67.

24 See "On the Origin of the Work of Art: First Version" in Gunter Figal, ed., *The Heidegger Reader,* trans. Jerome Veith (Indiana University Press, 2009), 130ff.

25 Heidegger, *Poetry, Language, Thought*, ibid., 148.

26 Paul M. Sammon, ibid., 92.

Kowalski's Apartment

27 See Peter L. Hays, *The Limping Hero: Grotesques in Literature* (New York University Press, 1971).

28 See, for instance, Joseph Campbell, *The Masks of God: Primitive Mythology* (NY: Penguin, 1987), 301.

29 See also Joseph Campbell, *The Masks of God: Oriental Mythology* (NY: Pengin, 1987), 169.

30 See the essay, "How Gilgamesh Became the Lord of the Dead" in John David Ebert, *Rage and the Word: Gilgamesh, Akhenaton, Moses and the Birth of the Metaphysical Age* (Eugene, OR: Post Egoism Media, 2014), 21ff.

31 Alain Badiou, *Being and Event*, trans. Oliver Feltham (London and New York: Continuum, 2007).

Chew's Eye Works

32 Paul M. Sammon, ibid., 135.

33 Ibid.,   133.

Rachael and Deckard

34 Gianni Vattimo, *A Farewell to Truth*, trans. William McCuaig (Columbia University Press, 2014).

35 See the essay on "Gerhard Richter" in John David Ebert, *Art After Metaphysics* (NY: Create Space, 2013), esp. 107-109.

Pris and J.F. Sebastian

36 Paul M. Sammon, ibid. 144 for "these walking mistakes that you've made."

Snake Scale

37 John Williamson, *The Oak King, the Holly King and the Unicorn: The Myths and Symbolism of the Unicorn Tapestries* (Olympic Marketing Corp, 1986). See also my review of Williamson's book in John David Ebert, *Texts: Collected Book Reviews from Joseph Campbell to Deleuze & Guattari* (NY: Create Space, 2015), 85ff.

38 See the essay "Christian Boltanski" in John David Ebert, *Art After Metaphysics*, ibid., esp. 209.

39 Paul M. Sammon, ibid., 145-146.

Zhora

40 For the myths associated with Inanna and her sister Ereshkigal, see Diane Wolkstein and Samuel Noah Kramer,

Inanna: Queen of Heaven and Earth, Her Stories and Hymns from Ancient Sumer (NY: Harper and Row, 1983).

41 Giorgio Agamben, ibid.1-4.

42 For Heidegger's concept of "world" vs. "worldlessness" see his early lecture, Martin Heidegger, *Towards the Definition of Philosophy*, trans. Ted Sadler, (London and New York: Continuum, 2008), 58-59.

Leon and Deckard

43 See Michel Foucault, *Discipline & Punish: the Birth of the Prison*, trans. Alan Sheridan (NY: Vintage Books, 1979), 192-194.

44 Zygmunt Bauman, *Liquid Modernity* (Cambridge and Oxford: Polity Press, 2000).

45 For an interesting reading of this poem see the chapter entitled "The Command from the Stone: Rilke's Experience," in Peter Sloterdijk, *You Must Change Your Life: On Anthropotechnics*, trans. Wieland Hoban (Cambridge, UK and Malden, MA: Polity Press, 2013), 19ff.

Rachael and Deckard (Redux)

46 See F.W.J. Schelling, *Investigations Into the Nature of Human Freedom*, trans. Jeff Love and Johannes Schmidt (State University of New York, 2006).

47 For this myth, see Samuel Noah Kramer, *The Sumerians: Their History, Culture and Character* (University of Chicago Press, 1971), 162-163.

Pris, Sebastian and Roy

48 For an excellent discussion of the symbolism of the egg as "arche," see J.J. Bachofen, *Myth, Religion and Mother Right,* trans. Ralph Mannheim, (Princeton, N.J.: 1967), esp. 24-30.

49 See "The Soul's Death Pole" in Jean Gebser, *The Ever-Present Origin*, trans. Noel Barstad and Algis Mickunas (Ohio University Press, 1985), 205ff.

Tyrell

50 For my concept of the metaphysical vulva, see " Introduction to the Metaphysical Vulva" in John David Ebert, *Alien Scene-by-Scene* (NY: Create Space, 2015), 11ff.

51 For an account of Ptah's creation by the power of the Word, see Joseph Campbell, *The Masks of God: Oriental Mythology*, ibid., 88.

52 Paul M. Sammon, ibid., 177.

The "Retirement" of Pris

53 Paul M. Sammon, ibid., 59.

The Battle with Roy

54 Heiner Muhlmann, MSC, Maximal Stress Cooperation, The Driving Force of Cultures (NY: Springer-Verlag, 2005).

55 Adriaan T. Peperzack, ed. Emmanuel Levinas: Basic Philosophical Writings (Indiana University Press, 1996).

Epilogue: Escape to the Countryside

56 As in Jean Gebser's sense of the gradual awakening of human consciousness historically speaking, whereas Deckard recapitulates it on the level of the individual. See Gebser's discussion of "The Three European Worlds" in *The Ever-Present Origin*, ibid., 9ff. The Sacrifice.

Bibliography

Agamben, Giorgio. *Homo Sacer: Sovereign Power and Bare Life*. Trans. Daniel Heller-Roazen. Stanford University Press, 1998.

Bachofen, J.J. *Myth, Religion and Mother Right*. Trans. Ralph Mannheim. Princeton, N.J.: 1967.

Badiou, Alain. *Being and Event*. Trans. Oliver Feltham. London and New York: Continuum, 2007.

Baudrillard, Jean. *To Do Away With Freedom or, How Not to Escape One's Destiny or, Fatal Against Fractal or, This World Which Thinks Us*. Trans. Sylvere Lotringer. Los Angeles: Semiotexte, 2015.

Bauman, Zygmunt. *Liquid Modernity*. Cambridge and Oxford: Polity Press, 2000.

Campbell, Joseph. *The Masks of God: Primitive Mythology*. NY: Penguin, 1987.

___. *The Masks of God: Oriental Mythology*. NY: Penguin, 1987.

___. ed. *The Portable Jung*. NY: Viking Penguin, 1971.

Dick, Philip K. *Do Androids Dream of Electric Sheep?* NY: Ballantine Del Rey, 2007.

Ebert, John David. *Alien Scene-by-Scene*. NY: Create Space, 2015.

___. *Art After Metaphysics*. NY: Create Space, 2013.

___. *Cultural Decay Rate: Essays on Contemporary Art, Literature and Social Disintegration*. NY: Create Space, 2015.

___. *Rage and the Word: Gilgamesh, Akenaton, Moses and the Birth of the Metaphysical Age*. Eugene, OR: Post Egoism Media, 2014.

___. *Texts: Collected Book Reviews from Joseph Campbell to Deleuze & Guattari*. NY: Create Space, 2015.

Figal, Gunter, ed. *The Heidegger Reader*. Trans. Jerome Veith. Indiana University Press, 2009.

Foucault, Michel. Discipline & Punish: the Birth of the Prison. Trans. Alan Sheridan. NY: Vintage Books, 1979.

Gebser, Jean. *The Ever-Present Origin*. Trans. Noel Barstad and Algis Mickunas. Ohio University Press, 1985.

Groys, Boris. *Art Power*. Cambridge, MA: MIT Press, 2008.

___. *Under Suspicion: A Phenomenology of Media*. Trans. Carsten Strathausen. Columbia University Press, 2012.

Hays, Peter L. *The Limping Hero: Grotesques in Literature*. New York University Press, 1971.

Heidegger, Martin. *Poetry, Language, Thought*. Trans. Albert Hofstadter. NY: Harper Perennial, 2001.

___. *Towards the Definition of Philosophy*. Trans. Ted Sadler. London and New York: Continuum, 2008.

Kennedy, Harlan. "Blade Runner: Ridley Scott Interviewed." http://www.americancinemapapers.com/files/blade-runner.htm

Kramer, Samuel Noah. *The Sumerians: Their History, Culture and Character*. University of Chicago Press, 1971.

Muhlmann, Heiner. *MSC, Maximal Stress Cooperation, The Driving Force of Cultures*. NY: Springer-Verlag, 2005.

Paglia, Camille. *Sexual Personae: Art and Decadence from Nefertiti to Emily Dickinson*. Yale University Press, 1990.

Peperzack, Adriaan, ed. *Emmanuel Levinas: Basic Philosophical Writings*. Indiana University Press, 1996.

Sammon, Paul M. *Future Noir: The Making of Blade Runner*. NY: Harper Prism, 1996.

Schelling, F.W.J. *Investigations Into the Nature of Human Freedom*. Trans. Jeff Love and Johannes Schmidt. State University of New York, 2006.

Schurmann, Reiner. *Broken Hegemonies*. Trans. Reginald Lilly. Indiana University Press, 2003.

Sloterdijk, Peter. *Spheres, Volume 2: Globes, Macrospherology*. Trans. Wieland Hoban. Los Angeles: Semiotexte, 2014.

___. *You Must Change Your Life: On Anthropotechnics*. Trans. Wieland Hoban. Cambridge and Malden: Polity Press, 2013.

___. and Hans-Jurgen Heinrichs. *Neither Sun Nor Death*. Trans. Steve Corcoran. Los Angeles: Semiotext, 2011.

Spengler, Oswald. *The Decline of the West*, trans. Charles Francis Atkinson. NY: Alfred A. Knopf, 1939.

Thompson, William Irwin. *Pacific Shift*. NY: Random House, 1986.

Vattimo, Gianni. *A Farewell to Truth*. Trans. William McCuaig. Columbia University Press, 2014.

Williamson, John. *The Oak King, the Holly King and the Unicorn: The Myths and Symbolism of the Unicorn Tapestries*. Olympic Marketing Corp, 1986.

Wolkstein, Diane and Kramer, Samuel Noah. *Inanna: Queen of Heaven and Earth, Her Stories and Hymns from Ancient Sumer*. NY: Harper and Row, 1983.

61482212R00083

Made in the USA
Lexington, KY
12 March 2017